Wine Tasting in Southern California & Beyond

Your guide to celebrating and exploring
So Cal's unique wineries, wine bars,
restaurants and more.

Janene Roberts

With over 70 wineries listed

3rd Edition

Additional copies of this book can be ordered
using the form in the back of this book.

Information in this book was researched and edited.
All information is accurate as of press time,
but may have since changed.
Popcorn Press & Media and Janene Roberts are not responsible
for discrepancies or changes.

Published in 2009 by Popcorn Press & Media.
P.O. Box 3375
Rancho Santa Fe, CA 92067

Book design & layout by Ellen Goodwin of Ellen Goodwin Graphics.
Edited by Andrea Glass of WritersWay
Map illustrations by Janene Roberts
Copyright © 2009 Janene Roberts.

First published in 1999.

ISBN 978-0-9674351-2-1
Printed in the United States of America

Dedicated to the hardworking wine owners and makers who combine their work in the soil with the artistry of winemaking to create wines we can enjoy for years to come. You inspire me with your down-on-your knees hard work combined with the beauty of your creations.

Acknowledgments

The Southern California wine landscape has changed substantially since the first edition of this book. The first edition listed 30 wineries. This version has over 70 wineries and a common statement while I was traveling to research this book was, "Oh by the way, do you know about the new winery that's opening up..." At some point I had to decide to say "that's a wrap" and so if you discover new wineries while you're out traveling with this book I wouldn't be surprised.

I'm grateful to the many people who have come along to support the new version of *Wine Tasting in San Diego & Beyond,* which is now being called *Wine Tasting in Southern California & Beyond.* I get more support each time I venture out to do an update and believe me this support helps the process of undertaking a project like this. Oh, you thought I just sat around tasting wine and lounging did you? Yeah, it'd be nice if the book wrote itself.

There are many people who came along to help. Mike Bragg of Taste of Wine TV produced a wonderful TV interview with Frank Mangio that was placed on his half hour TV show in San Diego and then re-ran it online. In addition, I'd like to thank Frank Mangio, wine columnist, for his support, and all the wineries, restaurants, wine bars and venues that opened their arms and made me feel welcome at their establishments. Also, thank you Linda Kissam for your hospitality and help.

My mother, who is a teetotaler, sold the last edition to people at her church! I've also had friends help sell the books. For the first time, companies have offered sponsorship money to help cover the costs of producing a project like this. A big thanks to:

Antelope Valley Wine Association, Hacienda de la Rosas, Orfila Winery, Seabreeze, Warner Springs Ranch, Malibu Family Wines, and Temecula Creek Inn.

Never did sun more beautifully steep
In his first splendor, valley, rock or hill;
Ne'er saw I, never felt, a calm so deep!

- William Wordsworth

Disclaimer

This book provides information regarding wine tasting in and around Southern California. The purpose is to provide information that is helpful to the wine enthusiast who lives in or travels to Southern California. It is intended to be a fun guide used for leisure activities. You should read and learn as much as possible and then use the information that is best for your needs. You may also want to read other texts to increase your knowledge. See the "For Further Reading" section.

Wine tasting takes time and patience to learn. For many people, the learning process is very enjoyable.

The contents of *Wine Tasting in Southern California & Beyond* have been edited and proofread to make it as accurate as possible. In addition, this information is accurate up to the printing date, but some information may have since changed. Please use this book as a guide and not as a final source of wine tasting information. While planning your trip you may want to verify the information with the establishment you intend to visit.

Popcorn Press & Media and the author are not liable or responsible for any loss or damage both alleged or caused either directly or indirectly by the contents of this book. It should be understood that the publisher and author do not provide health services or other related services. If these services are required, a professional should be sought. Also, remember to drink and drive responsibly. Designate a driver for your trip.

Contents

FREE NEWSLETTER

Here's an added benefit for you. Sign up for my free e-newsletter, Wine Girl Says at: https://app.e2ma.net/app/view%3AJoin/signupId%3A23800 or go to www.popcornpressmedia.com. Click on the Wine Tasting tab. Scroll down to "Subscribe now".

You'll get stories about my latest finds, excursions and fun stuff to do here in the Southern California Wine Region.

Introduction

This third edition marks the tenth year I've written about the Southern California winery region. I've seen so many changes in the wine scene here. The most notable being that the wines produced are gaining recognition for their quality. Most wineries have received at least one medal for their productions if they've submitted their wines to competitions. Also, more areas are in the process or have received their own appellation (AVA) status. An appellation can be the name of a vineyard, county or district. It defines where the grapes are grown. If a California wine label states an appellation, it must consist of at least 85 percent of wine from that area. Ramona, Malibu, Leona Valley and South Coast all have new appellations.

I've also found that wine enthusiasts are usually food enthusiasts too, so I've added more coverage of restaurants and specialty food stores along the winery paths. In addition, you'll find recipes from some of the wineries and restaurants that are included here. I think you'll like their contributions and suggested wine pairings.

I'd like to emphasize the importance of supporting your local community artisans. Many times, you'll be poured a tasting by the winemaker or owner himself when you visit. These artisans are creating art with their wines and foods they're making.

The editorials listed in this book are an unbiased opinion by the author. The author reports about the winery but hopes that the reader will make his own decision about the places he'd like to visit.

My goal with this book is to give readers ideas about where to go to experience wineries they may not have known about. It's also a celebration of the talented men and women who are creating unique wine and food in Southern California. More people are getting comfortable with the wine tasting experience. I still stress that what you should always remember when you're tasting wine is that you are the expert of your own tastes; that's what wine tasting is all about. The more you taste and experience, the more you'll realize what you enjoy and that's what your ultimate goal should be. Get ready to discover this expanding grape land.

A Love Affair

This is a story about love. Not love in the romantic sense but love of the open land, love of beauty, love of hard work and love of art.

Wine, and the people who make it, grow it and support it, is all that and more. It's a product to be enjoyed for what goes into the process. It's not a drink that's quickly sucked down. It's subtlety and appreciation. It's hands that pick grapes. It's letting the years pass while the juice ages to perfection. It's relaxing by the fire to wait a bit while the wine sits in the glass opening up to an even better product. This drink is not for the rushed. Patience is key.

I've found that wine appreciation slowly grows like a seed that's planted in the soil. At first you forget about it. Yes, you might remember planting it, but you don't really notice until the green shoots start popping up. That's when you start seeing its potential.

Maybe your friend dragged you to a wine tasting a few years ago, and you had a pretty good time. The people there were attractive. The wine was pretty good but you couldn't really tell the difference between the wines you tasted. And, maybe you felt a little intimidated by how others around you were describing the wine.

"Look at the legs," you heard a man to the left of you say.

"Beautiful aroma," a lady to the right of you commented. You looked at your friend and shrugged. You really didn't think about wine much after that until another friend took you to a blind wine tasting party at a friend's house. Again, you felt a little unsure of yourself but also were reminded you had gotten through the last wine tasting. At the blind wine tasting you started noticing differences in the wine as the host suggested ways to look for things like the color and how it sat in the glass. You even felt like you got the answers right when some of the others had the same comments that you wrote down in your tasting notes.

You picked one wine as your favorite and when the wines were revealed you were pleasantly surprised that it wasn't the most expensive one. You could even buy it at Costco. Your seed had shot out of the ground and you were growing.

I started this love affair about 13 years ago when my then husband and I were looking for something to do one day and decided to visit some of the Temecula wineries. Back then, only the original pioneers were there like Hart, Thornton, Callaway and Mount Palomar. Chardonnay and Cabernet Sauvignon were the main wines available for tasting but my seed had been planted. It would continue to grow through three evolutions of this book. Sometimes I look back at my naïveté in writing the first edition of this book. I wasn't taken very seriously by many of the wine people that I've grown to admire. But then, neither were many of the wineries I covered. I smile when I think of the evolution we've all taken.

Most of the winery owner's have decided to make a stake in the wine business for love. For some of them, that love means getting back to nature. For others, it's leaving a legacy for their families. Still others may just want more time right now with their families. Most of the wineries are small, family run operations—whether it's a couple or a 12-person family. But, in the end they're all working to create a product of beauty, hard work, science and art for people like you and me.

Community Building

So, how can you create this kind of beauty in your everyday life? You can experience it while you're touring the wineries, but I think there's a way to take it home with you too. You can buy the wine for your dinner party from your local winery or buy a case of wine at one of your favorite wineries while you're out touring and tasting.

You can also start building a community by inviting your family members to Sunday dinner or if your family's not in town, invite your friends and neighbors. You can also learn to grown your own herbs and vegetables. If you don't have land, grow plants in the window of your apartment. Having an appreciation for what goes into your body and where it came from is key.

The buzz word "sustainability" keeps popping up lately. I've talked with winemakers, looked up the meaning on the Internet and read various definitions of the word. I believe what it comes down to is taking a more conscious approach to life and realizing that everything we do contributes to either the benefit or the demise of our world and specifically our community.

I had a talk with the executive chef at the Ritz Carlton in Laguna Beach and he told me that he and his family had decided to put raised plant beds (four—one for each family member) in place of their front lawn. They each tend to their own beds. More seeds, literally, growing.

Since I live in a community that has a homeowner association, I've placed my plants in the backyard. There, you'll find a riot of herbs like lavender, rosemary, thyme, chives and parsley. Strawberries are growing on a hill and there are apple, avocado and orange trees, as well as tomatoes and garlic. I still want to plant more. You don't need a huge plot of land to do this. I live in a newer home in San Diego, where the fact that I have two side yards and enough space to put a dining table and chairs in the back yard is a big deal. And, you don't have to make it a big project. Start small. Join a community-supported agriculture (CSA) program. Go to a Slow Food meeting. See discussion below. Buy organic produce at the grocery. Support restaurants that offer local wine and produce. Take a weekend trip to the local wine country rather than flying hours away.

I got into this sustainability idea a while ago when I decided I'd make my home green. I bought a book on how to make your own green cleaning products (they didn't work very well) and probably stressed myself out more than I had to. Then I bought a composter and failed miserably at it. Did I say I tried to do all this while also renovating a home?

There are lots of small actions you can do now to make a difference in your community. And, please, stop whining about the lower quality of products that are in your local neighborhood. Are you really sure about that? I don't know how many times I've had to list gold medals from local wineries, which is why I list them in this book, to make people realize that places beyond Napa and Sonoma are making quality wines in California. Don't you like supporting the underdogs anyway?

Community Supported Agriculture (CSA)

Community supported agriculture, typically called CSA, is a program where customers buy shares or subscriptions of a local farmer's production and then either have the food delivered or mostly customers pick up the weekly or bi-weekly box of produce at an established location. The box may consist of vegetables and fruit or one or the other. The system benefits the customer by offering fresh, usually organic, produce and the farmer by insuring their production gets purchased. Most CSAs offer small shares feeding about two adults and large shares feeding about four adults for a week.

I've tried a bi-weekly share where I picked up the produce at a house that was as close to mine that I could find. I found the amount of produce I received was a little too much for one person and I would've preferred to find a place closer to pick up the produce. I've started using a CSA that delivers directly to my home. I love eating fresh produce. I snack on tomatoes and find unique recipes to make dishes like swiss chard and beets. I also feel very healthy and find that I naturally eat more vegetables without even trying.

Prices average between $25 and $40 a week to buy shares. Please check with each CSA to make sure they have drop offs in your area. Sometimes locations change or are added. Usually a home or business volunteers to be a drop off location.

You might want to consider touring some of these farms as well. Most of the farms would be glad to show you around.

INLAND EMPIRE

Sage Mountain Farm and De Luz Farms (951) 693-0272
www.inlandempirecsa.com
Offers locally grown organic fruit and vegetables in full and half sizes. Delivers to areas like Aguanga, Temecula, Riverside, Claremont, Loma Linda, Blue Jay, Hemet, Idyllwild and Anza. Customer picks up.

Tierra Miguel Foundation (760) 742-4213 www.tierramiguelfarm.org. Offers certified organic produce. Drop off locations at Murrieta, Riverside and Redlands.

LOS ANGELES

Tierra Miguel Foundation (760) 742-4213 www.tierramiguelfarm.org. Offers certified organic produce. Drop off locations at Long Beach, Torrance, Manhattan Beach, Mar Vista, Cheviot Hills, Westside JCC, Valley Village, Van Nuys, Granada Hills, Woodland Hills, Wonderland, Claremont, Pasadena, Sierra Madre, San Marino, Highland Park, Echo Park, Burbank, Glendale, La Canada and Altadena.

ORANGE COUNTY

Garden of Eden (760) 994-5861 www.goeorganics.com. One of the CSAs that offers a single person supply as well as small and large boxes. Drop points are Irvine and Tustin. Customer picks up.

Tierra Miguel Foundation (760) 742-4213 www.tierramiguelfarm.org. Offers certified organic produce. Drop off locations at San Clemente, Newport Beach and Costa Mesa.

OC Organics (949) 922-2501 www.ocorganics.com. Supplies fresh, locally grown produce that is delivered to your home or office. They cover South Orange County and North San Diego.

SAN DIEGO

Be Wise Ranch (760) 746-6006 www.bewiseranch.com. A certified organic farm including both vegetables and fruit in their boxes and offering small and large shares. Customers pick up shares in Hillcrest, La Mesa, Grossmont/La Mesa East, State College, North Park, Mission Hills, Solana Beach, Pacific Beach, South Kensington, Encinitas, Leucadia, Carlsbad, Vista, Escondido, Rancho Bernardo, Poway, Scripps Ranch, Mira Mesa, Tierrasanta and Clairemont.

Garden of Eden (760) 994-5861 www.goeorganics.com. One of the CSAs that offers a single person supply as well as small and large boxes. Drop locations at Hillcrest, Carlsbad/Encinitas, UCSD Campus, La Mesa, Rancho Bernardo, Solana Beach, Encinitas, Oceanside and Fallbrook.

OC Organics (949) 922-2501 www.ocorganics.com. Supplies fresh, locally grown produce that is delivered to your home or office. They cover South Orange County and North San Diego.

Seabreeze Organics (858) 481-0209 www.seabreezed.com. An organic farm that delivers to your home and includes a flower bouquet with the shipment. Small and large boxes available. Delivers throughout San Diego. Please check their website for zip codes.

Tierra Miguel Foundation (760) 742-4213 www.tierramiguelfarm.org. Offers certified organic produce with pick up locations at Pauma Valley, Valley Center, Escondido, SDSU, SD Waldorf School, Downtown San Diego, Pacific Beach, La Jolla, Clairemont and Del Mar.

Slow Food www.slowfoodusa.org

The Slow Food movement was started in 1989 by a man named Carlo Petrini. Petrini came up with the idea for Slow Food after a McDonald's restaurant opened on the Spanish Steps in Rome. It was primarily a wine and food association.

According to the book *Slow Food* (Petrini is the author), Slow Food began as a "gastronomic organization developed to rediscovering and protecting the right to enjoying the pleasures of the table and to using our tastebuds as guides to seeking the highest achievements in taste."

In 1996, the movement shifted its attention from gastronomy to ecology. This put the focus more on the land and farmers who produce fine artisanal foods. Thus, it became important to know where the food came from, who produced it and how to secure a future for its existence. The movement concentrates on holding tastings, educational workshops and major food events. There are Slow Food movements throughout Southern California. Check their website for one near you.

Wine Tasting Techniques

Tasting wine can be an overwhelming experience, especially if you're just beginning. But there are really only a few steps to remember. Keep in mind that tasting wine involves your senses: your eyes, nose, and mouth. The label will tell you the wine grape variety and vintage.

Try the following steps next time you're tasting wine. It should take you only a few minutes. Write down your impressions in the "Tasting Notes" section at the back of this book.

1. Color

Look at the color of the wine while it's in the glass. It should be clear with no film. But don't worry about sediment in red wines and crystals in white wines. These won't hurt you. Also, look at the hue of the wine. The darker the wine, the stronger the taste. However, as red wines get older the reverse is true. Be leery of red wines that are a true red or have hints of orange. Most likely they're too old. White wines are probably too old if there are hints of brown in them. White wines tend to get darker as they age. A good way to see the hue of the wine is to look at it against a white background. Tilt the glass and use a white cloth or paper to look at the wine near the outer edge of the glass.

2. Smell

This is an important step because your nose can detect thousands of scents. You should first swirl the wine. This will bring out the wine's bouquet. Now breathe in the wine and linger for just a moment. If you're using the back of this book to record your tasting, make a few notes about what you smell. Most often you will smell pleasant odors such as oak, honey, rose petals, and berries. However, you may also smell unpleasant odors. Sulfur dioxide, a burning match smell, is sometimes found in inexpensive white wines. Also, watch out for wine that has a vinegar smell. If you like what you smell, you'll most likely enjoy the taste. Don't worry about what it's "supposed" to smell like–everyone has different impressions.

3. Taste

Take a sip of the wine. Some people suggest moving the wine around in the mouth and holding it in the mouth for about ten seconds. This will give you an idea of how the wine tastes and feels. Do what you are comfortable with. As you sip, hold the wine on your tongue to determine if it is sweet, sour, salty, or bitter. Saltiness is difficult to detect; sweetness is probably the easiest. Usually white and rosé wines are the sweetest. A bitter wine will have an astringent taste. That's because it contains tannin, which is found in red wine. Tannin is an antioxidant that slows down the aging cycle of red wine. It is found in grape skins, stalks, and sometimes in oak barrels. If a wine is too bitter, try eating some cheese. This will help to reduce the bitter flavor because the protein in the cheese will mix with the tannin and soften the taste. Try "chewing" the wine as you would chew food. You might find different tastes by doing this. Once you've swallowed the wine, note the lingering taste. This is called the "length."

Try to determine why you like one wine over the other, and while you're tasting, note the differences in expensive versus inexpensive wines. It's a good idea to drink water after each taste to clear your palate.

Interested in taking a class on wine tasting? Try the Balboa Park (San Diego) Food & Wine School. The school is in the House of Hospitality and offers wine classes with titles such as "Forget the Wine Geeks, Wine is for Everyone." Contact the school for more information: (619) 557-9441 or www.balboafoodwine.com.

Starting a Wine Tasting Group

One of the best ways to learn about wine is to taste it with a group. Many beginners are often intimidated by wine tasting groups, but being in a group where everyone is a willing learner can really forge a path to understanding. If you currently aren't part of a wine tasting group, this chapter will give you some ideas about forming your own (or helping a friend start one).

The group that I taste wine with starts with eighteen people and eight bottles of wine. Getting enough people to help share the cost allows the group to purchase wine that's more expensive than you'd perhaps buy on your own. However, the size of the group isn't as important as the consistency of its meeting. The group I taste with meets once a month. Find people who show an interest in tasting wine, starting with friends, family, and co-workers. Pretty soon you'll be turning folks away.

Although my group uses a form to score wines, you don't have to be that formal. You'll need to pay attention to the wine characteristics in order to take notes and describe what you're tasting, but you can make the tasting rather loose and just talk about it.

According to an article in the magazine *Wine Country Living* (June 2002), a couple in Napa Valley, including Schramsberg winemaker Hugh Davies, have informal three-vintage Sunday tastings and start with the youngest vintage wines first. Like the group I taste with, the Schramsbergs usually sample eight wines at a time and usually have a theme such as "American Pinot Noir" or "Napa Valley Cabernet."

Here are some quick tips to help you get started:

1. Gather a group of people. Eighteen people can conduct an eight-bottle tasting.

2. Buy pouring spouts for your wine bottles. I bought mine at WineSellar & Brasserie. The spouts pour out accurate amounts of wine to allow for approximately eighteen tastes per standard-sized bottle (750 ml).

3. Figure out where and when to meet.

4. Ask each person to bring the appropriate number of wineglasses, or supply enough glasses yourself.

5. Pick a leader (it will probably end up being you if you're organizing the group).

6. Decide on a topic and determine how much the group members want to spend. The group I taste with chooses topics based on wines from a particular region or a single grape variety.

7. Establish judging criteria. My group uses the U.C. Davis 20-point rating scale. Decide if you want to blind taste or not. The group I taste with conducts blind tastings: each participant chooses his or her top three samples, the wines are then unveiled, and the group finds out which wines got the most points. Sometimes the low-cost wines are the favorites.

I've found that tasting wine is sort of like going to college: the more educated you are, the more you want to learn. But regardless of how you set up your tastings, remember to taste wine regularly with the group, and enjoy yourself! Cheers!

If you're not interested in organizing the wine tasting, try calling 1-800-WineShop. According to their literature, this company will bring you a half-case of wines selected from over 200 boutique vineyards—and they'll also conduct the entire tasting.

Benefits of Wine

In May 1990, an article appeared in HEALTH Magazine that addressed the "French paradox." Even more people heard about this issue on a 60 Minutes television segment based on the article. The basis of the paradox was that French people (who consume a lot of cheese, meat, butter, and red wine) have half the death rate from heart disease as that of Americans. The study concluded that people who drink in moderation–two glasses each day–develop heart disease less frequently than people who don't drink at all and people who drink heavily. This new, hopeful information gave people a reason to stock up on their wine supplies. Then medical researchers declared that wine was not only good for you, but all kinds of alcoholic beverages were good for you. They maintained that the alcohol in the drinks kept arteries unclogged because it raised HDL cholesterol levels and kept the blood from clotting. However, in 1995 a Copenhagen heart study found that the effect of beer on mortality rates was minimal and liquor's effect was actually connected to increased heart disease rates. It found that regular wine drinkers had the least instance of heart disease.

Another study, conducted at the University of California at San Diego School of Medicine, determined that the lowest amount of heart disease was found among people in countries that had the highest rate of wine consumption. Researchers also found that the lowest heart disease rates occurred where people ate a great deal of fruit. The idea stems from the presence of phenolic flavonoids found in wine's non-alcoholic compounds (natural antioxidants). Phenolic flavonoids are found in the skin, seeds, and stems of red grapes. Antioxidants are believed to be one factor that protects bodies from oxidation.

Oxidation of LDL cholesterol may lead to artery blockage and heart attacks. Thus, phenolics may disrupt this pattern.

Fresh fruits have a high concentration of phenolics and wine, after the fermentation of grapes, has an increased concentration of the chemical. Red wine has an exceptional amount of phenolics because it contains whole-fruit extracts.

However, some people are still skeptical of these findings and note that alcoholic drinks are associated with other health risks. These include esophageal, throat, and mouth cancers, liver disease, and breast cancer. But these risks may be associated with the actual alcohol content of the drinks; some experts say that the phenolic antioxidants of wine counter these problems.

People are drinking wine more frequently in part because it has been proven to raise HDL cholesterol, and thins the blood a little. Supposedly, these factors protect against heart disease.

However, do not think of wine as a cure-all; rather, it should be something to enjoy and used with restraint.

In any event, as the experts research the facts, the best advice is to drink in moderation and remember to drink responsibly and designate a driver for the ride home. So, sit back, relax, and enjoy one to two glasses of wine each day.

Serving Wine

Some people believe that each wine requires its own unique glass. The reason is that the shape of the glass determines how the wine is received on the tongue. It is recommended that red wines, especially those that are young, be drunk out of glasses that have larger bowls with rims that have a slender inward curve to keep the wine from spilling. The larger bowls allow swirling of the wine, which causes aeration. Most people, however, do not have a large collection of glasses. Your best bet is to purchase good all-purpose wineglasses with 10- to 12-ounce bowls.

When you are at a restaurant and ordering a nice-quality wine, make sure the waiter gives you appropriate glasses and fills the glass half full so that there is enough room for swirling. If you order an expensive bottle of wine and the waiter brings out small-bowled glasses, ask if more appropriate glasses are available. Otherwise, you're better off ordering a less expensive bottle since you won't be able to distinguish the variations of aroma and taste with small-bowled glasses.

If you're at a restaurant and a waiter gives you the cork of the wine you ordered, don't sniff it—check for intactness, not scent. However, many corks are now made of plastic instead of cork because the natural ones can leak or fall apart. To stay with tradition, a lot of the higher-priced wines continue to use cork. It remains to be seen if all wine corks will become plastic.

Here are some suggestions for serving wine at home:
- Wash your wineglasses by hand using hot water and a small amount of soap. Then dry the glasses by hand for sparkling stemware.

- Store wineglasses with their bowls facing up so that the rims do not carry the smell of your cupboard.
- Wine can sometimes taste better in thin glasses that have lean rims.
- Youthful wines need large glasses to help tannin emanate.
- Remember to hold the wineglass by the stem. It is possible that the heat from your hand placed on the bowl could affect the wine's temperature.
- Fill the glass no more than half full to allow room for swirling.
- Serve water with wine to allow for cleansing of the palate.
- When serving various bottles of wine, start with a young wine and then move on to an older one. If you are serving whites and reds, start with whites and progress to reds. Other considerations include starting with a light wine and moving on to a more robust one as well as starting with a dry wine and moving on to a sweeter one.
- White wines should be chilled about a half hour before serving. Cold white wines should be taken out of the refrigerator 20 minutes prior to drinking. After the desired temperature is reached, put the white wine in a temperature-controlled wine urn.
- If you would like to chill red wine, chill it for 20 minutes just before drinking it.
- Wine that you have leftover can be stored in the refrigerator with the cork back in but complex wines won't last as long as less complex ones, so generally the more expensive the wine, the better it is to drink it the day it was opened.

Wine History

Wine has been around for thousands of years. However, there is debate over how wine was first created. It has been said that archaeologists found grape seeds and winemaking tools in prehistoric caves and that traces of Egyptian vineyards have been found that go back to 3000 B.C. However, most historical evidence dates to about 1000 B.C. At that time, wine was introduced to Italy and France during the Greek Empire expansion. During the Roman Empire, the Romans mastered the process of aging wines and used barrels and bottles that are similar to the ones used today. As Romans occupied Europe, they brought their wines and vines with them. Some people credit the Romans for laying the groundwork for the famous French vineyards of today, including those in Provence, the Rhône Valley, Bordeaux, Burgundy, and Loire.

In the Middle Ages, the Roman Catholic Church took over the wine trade and monks began using wine for religious ceremonies as well as for recreation. During this time, the church owned a large number of vineyards in Europe. It was then that many of the terms and techniques used in winemaking today were formed.

In early America, Thomas Jefferson enjoyed wine and often went to France to purchase wine for himself and George Washington, James Madison, James Monroe, and John Quincy Adams. When Jefferson was the U.S. Ambassador to France, he explored the wine regions of Europe. In the 1770s he invested in The Wine Company, which produced wine, oil, and silk.

Amazingly, California's most infamous events, earthquakes, are what actually make the state such a prime place for growing grapes. The soil becomes richer as the earth's plates grind together. As different soils are created, they make varied growing conditions. Therefore, the more varieties of soil, the more varieties of wine can be produced through planting different grapes in different soils.

As Southern California continues to grow in population, so does the number of vineyards. However, the population changes through the years have changed the locations of wine regions.

San Diego was the first Southern California area to grow grapes for winemaking. Some people say that it was Franciscan missionary Father Junipero Serra who planted the vines in 1769 at the Mission San Diego de Alcala. Other people debate that assertion. The missionaries traveled from Baja California and established twenty-one missions and planted what was called the mission grape variety for sacramental and medicinal uses. The missionaries were the only viticulturists in California for about 60 years. In the 1820s, the first commercial grower was Joseph Chapman in the Los Angeles area and then in 1831 the Frenchman Jean Louis Vignes brought the first vines from Europe to Southern California. Now, instead of a vineyard, that area has become downtown Los Angeles.

With the Gold Rush came a greater desire for wine and the local winemakers soon had competition from many European winemakers.

In the 1850s a man named Agoston Haraszthy went to Europe and came back with 100,000 vine cuttings, which made a large impact on the number of grape varieties winemakers could use. He brought European varieties to Southern California and later moved to Sonoma, where his vines adapted easily. His contributions were the beginnings of the transformation from the mission grape to the European varieties.

By the end of the 1800s, quite a few Europeans had established wineries in California. The industry was hit with Prohibition two decades later and only a few wineries endured (by manufacturing wines for religious ceremonies or growing grapes for home winemaking use). Many wineries had to start all over again once Prohibition was repealed.

There was a demand for wine after Prohibition but the wines produced in California at that time were inferior to ones produced elsewhere. To maintain the status of California's wine industry, The

Wine Institute was developed in 1934. This institute helped organize quality and labeling guidelines. Today, The Wine Institute is based in San Francisco and serves as a public policy advocacy association for California wineries. From the 1930s until now the wine industry in California has grown and continues to show an expanding market.

In the 1980s the largest winery area near San Diego was the Cucamonga district between Ontario and Fontana in San Bernardino County. Unfortunately, human population also grew in this region and began pushing out the grape-growing areas. Thus, several vineyards opened in Temecula (first called "Rancho California"), which was south of the Cucamonga district, north of Escondido, and only about an hour's drive from the mission in San Diego.

Shipping Wine

Many people don't know that some states don't allow shipment of wine. So, it's important that you know if you can legally ship that Orfila Syrah you're planning to send to Aunt Martha in Alabama. There are **Reciprocal Agreements** (reciprocal means that the shipment of wine is allowed if the other state has the same agreement), **Restrictions/Special Agreements** (check with the individual state for specific rules) and **Prohibited Agreements** (don't send wine there). The good news is that the laws are quickly becoming more relaxed. Your best bet is to check with the winery you're purchasing the wine from to make sure you can mail it to the planned destination.

Grape Varieties

Did you know that the names of grape varieties have only appeared on bottles of California wines since the 1950s? Before that time, generic names were given to California wines that contained just one variety. In California, wineries now label their wines by the grapes from which they are made. Single varietals are wines made from one grape. When a wine is labeled "Chardonnay," it must consist of 75 percent of that grape variety. Single varietal wines are regarded as the best. However, they are not always an indication of quality. Since 1983, American Viticultural Areas (AVA) have begun to be established in California. An AVA is a type of appellation where winegrowers in certain areas will ask the government to grant them the right to put that area's name on their wine labels. If the right is granted, 85 percent of the wine in those bottles must be from that area.

Characteristics of grape varieties depend on local climates and customs, but for the most part, grape varieties are consistent. The two most important categories of California wines are varietal and generic.

Varietal wines contain at least 75 percent of one variety of grape and are named after that grape. Generic wines are a blend of different grapes. You may find that a number of bottles are labeled "Meritage." This means that the wine combines Bordeaux varieties like Cabernet Sauvignon and Merlot.

Another name found on labels is a proprietary name. Wineries may label their wines with this name for marketing purposes. The proprietary name used to be on the label instead of a generic name, but now the proprietary name is being used instead of a varietal name for the winery's best wines.

An article in the *San Diego Union-Tribune* in August 2002 mentioned that French scientists have charted the DNA of wine, and can now determine if the wine in a bottle matches its label. According to the article, this is the result of an increasing number of inexpensive wines being sold for far more than their worth. In France, the French government takes this offense seriously and in some cases will fine and imprison sellers of fraudulent wine.

The following are the most common types of varietals found when wine tasting in and near Southern California:

Aleatico

A red variety most often used to produce a dessert wine. The wines are often described as "sweet."

Barbera

A red variety that grows in Italy and California. It has a high acid level. The wines it produces are dry.

Cabernet Sauvignon

A red grape from Bordeaux, France, it produces a wine that is naturally high in tannin. It is produced into dry, red, white, and pink wines. Some people describe the wine as smelling of black currants, cassis, dried herbs, and bell pepper. Most connoisseurs describe it as having depth because it is more complicated than Merlot. Sometimes Merlot is mixed with this variety to add softness.

Carignane

A red grape from Southern France best grown in warm regions. It produces a dry red wine and is sometimes mixed with Grenache, Syrah, and Cinsault.

Chardonnay

A white grape from Burgundy that is very popular in California. It produces a white wine with moderate acidity, which is often aged in oak barrels; therefore, almost all of these wines have an oak taste. The wine can smell of grass and herbs. It is often described as having earth flavors, hints of melon and fig, and can achieve a high alcohol content. Other words to describe this wine include fruit, vanilla, and butter. It is often mixed with Sémillion.

Charbono

A red grape from Northern Italy. It produces a full-bodied, dry red wine. Only a few wineries grow this variety.

Chenin Blanc

A distinct white grape that was very popular for about 10 years, but its popularity has recently declined. It is grown mainly in California, Washington, and Texas. The Loire Valley in France produces Chenin Blancs that are different from the American versions. The French versions have a sharp, acidic taste and are called Vouvray (named after the district they come from in the Loire Valley). In the United States the taste of Chenin Blanc is primarily dry or semi-dry. These white wines tend to have a fruity taste and are sometimes produced widely and then made into a jug wine or a generic blend.

Cinsault

A large black grape that was formerly called Black Malvoisie. Only small amounts of this grape are grown in California. Most often it is blended with other wines to offset a high alcohol content.

Dolcetto

A red variety, the Dolcetto grape is purple and originally from the Piedmont region in Italy. The wine is meant to be drunk young and can be described as full, dry, and soft with a fruity taste.

French Colombard

A white variety that is planted extensively. It can produce wines that have some acidity and is often made into an inexpensive, dry white wine.

Fumé Blanc

Also known as Sauvignon Blanc.

Gamay/Napa Gamay

A red grape believed to be from Southern France. It produces light-to-medium-bodied wines that are dry and red or pink with a fruity taste. Most of the time they have either little or no oak aging (wine that sits in oak barrels) and are produced by a technique called carbonic maceration. Drink these wines when they are young, within about six months to a year of the vintage. This will keep the freshness of the fruit alive.

Gewürztraminer

A white variety that produces a dessert wine that is dry or medium dry. The grape is grown in cool regions. The wine has a spicy and flowery smell and is often described as "sweet" and "tart." It usually has an intense flavor and is generally low in alcohol. "Gewürz" means "spicy" in German.

Grenache/Grenache Rosé/White Grenache

A red grape variety from Southern France. The California variety produces wines that have hints of strawberry and citrus. The wine is light in color and is sometimes produced as a rosé. Wines the grape produces are usually dry and medium-dry or are pink or red in color.

Malbec

Malbec is a red wine with a medium to full body. The wine has been described as having blackberry and plum flavors. The color is usually dark purple with fruit and herbal aromas.

Merlot

A Bordeaux red variety that has been popular since the 1990s. The wines are sometimes described as having scents of chocolate, plum, and earth. Most people describe Merlot as smooth. Sometimes it is blended with Cabernet Sauvignon to add strength to its character. Merlots mature quicker than Cabernet Sauvignons and can be enjoyed as a younger wine. The wines produced are dry and pink or red and have moderate tannin.

Mourvèdre/Mataro

A red Mediterranean variety that is most often blended with other wines. California wines made from this varietal have an herbal character.

Muscat

Exists as both a red and white variety. The grape has aromatic characteristics that may be fruity, spicy, or floral. The grapes are often used to make dessert wines or Italian Spumante.

Nebbiolo

An Italian variety that produces wines that are dry red and also sweet pink.

Petite Sirah (Syrah)

A dark-skinned red variety, it produces a very dark red wine and sometimes produces a pink wine. The wines usually have a black pepper taste and aroma and can be jammy (a heavy, jam-like taste). The California variety really isn't a variety at all; it usually consists of four or more varieties. The wine has a good deal of tannin and is dry.

Petit Verdot

Petit Verdot produces a red wine often used in Bordeaux blends. Local wineries are beginning to produce the grape into a single varietal wine and it's showing promise. Some words used to describe the aroma and flavor of the wine include violet, leather, black currant, spice and bell pepper.

Pinot Grigio

Pinot Grigio is a white wine that originated in Northern France but is now associated with Italy which has been cultivating the grape for more than a century. The grape grows best in cooler regions with high mineral soils. This grape is most often best on its own and is known for its delicate, crisp, and white fruit flavors.

Pinot Gris

A red variety that is a variation of Pinot Noir. It produces a simple dry white wine.

Pinot Noir/Gamay Beaujolais

A red grape from the Burgundy region that is sometimes described as a grape with "personality" and "sensuality." It produces a red wine that is naturally low in tannin. It tends to be fruity, crispy, and with a light body. The wine can have the taste of spices and berries. Its color is lighter than red wines such as Merlot or Cabernet Sauvignon. For some time it wasn't very successful in California. That may be because it's hard to grow in the area. It thrives in areas that are low in temperature and overcast. The areas best suited for Pinot Noir grapes in California are places like Santa Barbara.

Riesling/Johannisberg Riesling/White Riesling

A white variety that tends to be fruity and floral. The grape has high acidity and thrives in a cool climate; it grows and matures slowly. It is grown in California, but tends to be milder than its cooler-region counterparts. The wine is more popular in Europe than in the United States. Most great Rieslings can be found in Germany, Austria, and Alsace, France.

White Riesling is a wine produced from grapes cultivated in California, while Johannisberg Riesling is named after grapes grown in Germany. The latter produces a dry to medium-dry white wine.

Sangiovese

A red grape from Italy. These wines tend to be a medium-red color and are often described as having hints of cherry or smoky flavors. Originally from Tuscany, Italy, this variety is becoming very popular in the hotter regions of California, such as the Temecula Valley. Results in Temecula so far have been promising. This grape produces the wine called Chianti. Chianti is meant to be drunk young and is sometimes mixed with other varieties.

Sauvignon Blanc/Fumé Blanc

A white variety that tends to be very acidic. This gives the wine a dry, crisp taste. Sauvignon is derived from the French word "sauvage," which means "savage" or "wild." Some people describe it as a stubborn wine. The wine can be sharp, brisk, and lively. Many American wines are a tamed-down version of the true Sauvignon Blanc because many winemakers feel that the true wine is too bold for Americans. In California some Sauvignon Blancs are called Fumé Blanc. These wines are declining in popularity in favor of Chardonnays. In warm regions, these white wines tend to have hints of spice, citrus, pear, and some earthy characteristics.

Sémillon

A white variety originally from the Bordeaux region in France. The grape produces a dry-to-sweet white wine. The wine has scents of spice and fig. It's often blended with Sauvignon Blanc; this combination is sometimes labeled "Meritage."

Syrah

A red variety from the Rhône Valley, France. Words used to describe the Rhône wines are "leathery," "damp," "robust," "earthy," "smoky," "pepper," and "spicy." The California Syrahs produce spicy dry red wines. This isn't the same variety as Petite Sirah, which produces a darker, tannic wine.

Tempranillo

A red variety from a black grape originally from Spain. The grape is often used to make Rioja wine. Most often, Tempranillo is aged in oak barrels and the varietal wine is often described as having aromas of berries, vanilla and herbs.

Viognier

A white variety from the Rhône Valley, France. This variety is showing great promise in the Temecula region. Sometimes the wine it produces is described as having tastes of peaches and apricots.

Zinfandel

A red grape that is one of the most widely planted in California. Zinfandel grapes are versatile and produce a dry red wine or rosé wine. Zinfandels are mostly a California variety because hardly any other wine region in the world grows it. There is debate over where the grape originated, but the consensus is that it is of European origin and of a variety called "vinifera." Cooler regions tend to produce a wine with distinguishable tastes of spice and berries. The grape produces a range of wines from light White Zinfandels to rich Zinfandels. They can be made into white wine or even sweet port.

Zinfandel wine is often confused with White Zinfandel wine. The biggest difference is that Zinfandel wines are red and White Zinfandel wines are pink. Zinfandel wines are often described as big and strong. Some people say that the best way to use a Zinfandel grape is to make a true Zinfandel. "Jammy" and "chewy" are sometimes used to describe this wine, and hints of blackberry, spice, and boysenberry can be detected.

White Zinfandel is a light-pink colored wine. Grapes used to produce this wine are picked earlier and have less color and sugar than the grapes used for red Zinfandel. The color of the wine is created by removing the red skins of the grapes before a deep color can be produced. This wine is often thought of as a young person's wine and is often not taken very seriously. Words used to describe this wine are "sweet" and "weak."

Wine and Food Pairings

You could read and study whole books about this subject but isn't it more fun just to dig in and try experimenting yourself? Besides, do you really want more rules around your food and wine? Sure there are basics you can go by, and I'll list those below, but I tend to learn best by experimenting. So, I've asked some of the wineries and restaurants that are a part of this book to supply recipes and suggest wine pairings. Get out your saute pan, grab some fresh lobster from your local fisherman and get to work!

Color

I'm sure you've already heard that white wines are supposed to go with white meats and red wines with red (a classic is the steak with Cabernet Sauvignon pairing) but there are a few more things to think about when pairing wine and food. And, sometimes red wines do go with white meats and vice versa.

So, it's not just about the color. Think about the character of the food and wine. You want both to complement each other. If the dish has subtle flavors you'd want to complement it with a subtle wine.

However, the wine and food shouldn't be too much alike or they won't bring out the differences in each other. In some instances contrasting characters can work together and bring about a whole new taste sensation. So, you could take a hot, spicy dish and combine it with a slightly sweet wine.

Style

Think about the personality of the dish and wine. If they have a similar style, most likely they'll be a good match. What's the structure or weight of the dish and wine? An acidic wine like Sauvignon Blanc goes well with creamy or cheesy dishes or meats like sausages.

The best food and wine match is one where both interact wonderfully to create an experience far beyond what either could develop alone.

Recipes

Thornton Winery's Café Champagne's Baked Brie Wrapped in Puff Pastry with Honey Walnut Sauce

Serve with Thornton 1996 Brut Reserve

2.2 pound wheel of brie, cut into 16 wedges
1 package frozen puff pastry dough (thawed)
2 sticks of butter or 8 ounces
4 ounces honey
1 teaspoon garlic, minced
1 tablespoon chopped parsley
1/4 cup chopped nuts

1. Roll out thawed puff pastry dough with rolling pin and divide into eight pieces.

2. Form a rectangle with the brie by using two pieces of brie and wrap the puff pastry around the cheese. Seal tightly with piece of puff pastry dough. Bake brie in puff dough at 400 degrees until golden brown, approximately 10 minutes.

3. Combine honey, butter and garlic in a sauce pan. Heat just until butter is melted. Place sauce on small plate, sprinkle with walnuts and parsley. Place cooked, wrapped brie on top. Serves 8

Ritz Carlton Laguna Niguel Wine and Cheese Tasting Plate with Orange Fig Marmalade, Roasted Grapes, and Candied Walnuts

Orange Fig Marmalade

  1 tablespoon butter
  2 shallots, minced
  2 cups fresh figs, quartered
  1 cup Port Wine
  2 naval oranges, juiced
  1 orange, zested
  Salt and pepper

Melt butter in medium pan and sauté the shallots until translucent. Add the figs, Port Wine, orange juice and zest. Cook over medium heat until the liquid is reduced by three quarters. Let cool and puree with a hand held emersion mixer. Season with salt and pepper.

Roasted Grapes

  1 large bunch of seedless red grapes
  Olive oil
  Salt and pepper

Toss the grapes with olive oil, salt and pepper. Place in an ovenproof dish and roast at 400 degrees for 6 to 8 minutes. Allow to cool.

Candied Walnuts

  2 cups walnuts, halved
  3 cups simple syrup (equal parts of sugar and water)
  1 cup powdered sugar

Blanch the walnuts in boiling simple syrup for a few minutes. Drain the nuts and dredge in the powdered sugar. Spread the nuts on a baking sheet and bake at 350 degrees for 8 to 10 minutes.

To assemble:

Fan the cheese slices (use any type of cheese you enjoy) on a wooden serving board. Garnish with the candied walnuts and roasted grapes. Serve the cheese with slices of olive bread and enjoy with the Orange Fig Marmalade.

Hacienda de las Rosas Barbeque Pork Ribs

This amazing dish will give you
a spicy taste for summer barbeques!

4-6 lbs of baby back ribs
4 teaspoons of Hacienda de las Rosas Mesquite Spices
salt/pepper
1 cup El Fuego wine (50% Petite Syrah / 50% Ruby Cabernet)

Wash the baby back ribs, place on broiling rack, and pour 1 cup of El Fuego wine across ribs. Hand rub spices on both sides of ribs, and slightly salt/pepper. Broil for approximately 20-25 minutes until brown.

Ponte Winery's Lobster Risotto

Serve with Ponte Fume Blanc

10 oz. arborio rice
2 tablespoons chopped shallots
1 tablespoon minced garlic
1 cup dry sherry
24 oz. lobster tail meat, cut into 1 inch pieces
lobster stock or clam juice, as needed
1 teaspoon finely chopped sage
2 cups heavy cream
1/2 cup shredded parmesan cheese
kosher salt & white pepper
1/2 cup canola oil

Heat canola oil in a heavy bottomed medium sauce pan. Add lobster, garlic and shallots and sauté for 30 seconds. Add sherry and cook until sherry evaporates. Remove the lobster from the pan and set aside. Add rice and enough stock or clam juice to just cover the rice. While stirring constantly, cook over medium heat until the liquid is mostly dried up. Add more liquid, enough to cover the rice again, and continue stirring over medium heat until dry again. Add heavy cream to just cover the rice. Stir in parmesan, sage, lobster, and salt and pepper. Cook for a minute or two, stirring constantly, until creamy. Serve immediately. Serves 6.

The Loft at Montage's Barbecued Sonoma Quail, Roasted Baby Eggplant and Housemade Pickles, Grape Butter

For the quail

6 each sonoma quail, chest cavity boned out

3 tablespoons barbecue sauce, of your choice, something sweet and spicy works best.

2 teaspoons kosher salt

For the garnish

5 each baby Japanese eggplants, cut into quarters

2 tablespoons grapeseed oil

1/4 cup golden raisins

1/2 cup white wine

1 tablespoon clover honey

1/2 teaspoon red curry paste

2 each housemade pickles, sliced thin. Kosher dill pickles may be substituted.

1 bunch frisee, cleaned from the stem

1 teaspoon olive oil

1 teaspoon lemon juice

2 teaspoons kosher salt

1 bunch Italian parsley, chopped fine

For the sauce

1 cup dry white wine

2 tablespoons white wine vinegar

1 stem of thyme

2 large shallots, sliced thin

1/2 cup heavy cream

1/2 pound unsalted butter, cubed and kept cold

10 each red grapes

1 1/2 teaspoons kosher salt

In a small sauce pan add the raisins, white wine, honey and curry from the garnish. Bring to a simmer and stir occasionally until the raisins are rehydrated. Reserve.

In a medium sized sauce pan add the shallots, thyme, white wine and vinegar. Simmer until ninety-five percent of the liquid is reduced. Add the cream and reduce by half. With a wire whisk, on low heat, slowly add the cubes of butter one at a time until all the butter has been incorporated. Crush the grapes into the sauce and whisk until incorporated. Finish with the salt. Reserve in a warm area (sauce will separate if it gets too cool or hot).

Heat your grill or barbecue to high heat. In a small bowl toss the quail with the barbecue sauce and salt. Grill on both sides to desired doneness (about ten minutes).

While the quail is cooking heat a large sauté pan to high heat. Add the grapeseed oil and heat for approximately 10 seconds. Add the eggplant and cook till golden brown on all sides and tender. Finish the eggplant with raisins, parsley and salt.

To serve, remove the quail from the grill and let rest for approximately three minutes. On individual plates place the eggplant mixture in the center and top with the quail. Drizzle the sauce around the plate. In a small bowl toss the frisee, olive oil, lemon juice and pickles together. Place the salad on top of the quail and serve. Serves 6.

Sapphire Laguna's
Pan-Seared Barramundi with
Market Vegetables and Tomato Confit

Chef/Owner Azmin Ghahreman of Sapphire Laguna

Pair with Bandol, Domaines Ott "Rosé Coeur de Grain" 2006

For the Tomato Confit:

4 Roma tomatoes, cored and halved

2 shallots, sliced

4 garlic cloves

2 sprigs fresh thyme

Olive oil, enough to cover

For the Market Vegetables:

6 asparagus spears, cut into 2-inch pieces

2 ounces snow peas

1/4 pound yellow wax beans, trimmed and cut in half

4 baby beets, cut in half

8 fingerling potatoes, cut in half

1/4 cup olive oil

1 teaspoon minced shallot

1 teaspoon chopped parsley

For the Barramundi:

1/3 cup grapeseed oil

Four (6-ounce) fillets barramundi with skin on

Salt and white pepper to taste

Herbes de Provence Butter (recipe below)

For Garnish:

4 lemon segments

Parsley sprigs

Preheat oven to 350 degrees Fahrenheit.

Place the tomato halves in a sauté pan with the garlic, sliced shallots and thyme. Add enough olive oil to cover the tomatoes and then cover completely with a piece of aluminum foil. Place in the oven until tomatoes are soft yet still hold their shape, about 30 minutes. Let cool and set aside.

Bring 2 quarts of water to a boil with salt (water should taste like the ocean) and prepare an ice water bath. Separately blanch the asparagus, snow peas and wax beans and then plunge in ice water to stop cooking. Cook the beets and potatoes in separate pots of salted boiling water until tender, about 15 minutes. Drain cooled vegetables and peel the skin off the beets when cool enough to touch. Set aside.

Adjust the oven temperature to 375 degrees Fahrenheit. Season the fish fillets with salt and white pepper. Heat the grapeseed oil in a large sauté pan over medium-high heat, place the fish skin side down and cook until crisp, about 2 minutes. Turn the fish over and cook for 2 more minutes. Add 2 tablespoons of Herbes de Provence Butter (recipe next page) to the top of each fillet and transfer to the oven to finish cooking, about 5 minutes.

Heat the olive oil in another sauté pan over medium-high heat. Sauté the fingerling potatoes until they begin to brown, then add the rest of the vegetables and the shallots. Cook until heated through. Season with salt and pepper to taste and then toss with the chopped parsley.

To serve, divide the vegetables onto four plates and place in a neat pile in the center of each. Add equal amounts of tomato confit to each plate and place the fish on top. Garnish with a lemon segment and a sprig of parsley. Serves 4.

Herbes de Provence Butter

1/4 pound (1 stick) sweet butter, softened
1 garlic clove, chopped
1 teaspoon chopped shallot
1 teaspoon Herbes de Provence
1 tablespoon hot water
Juice of 1/2 lemon
1/2 teaspoon lemon zest
2 teaspoons chopped fresh parsley
Dash of Tabasco
Pinch of salt
Pinch of white pepper

Mix all the ingredients together. If not using immediately, wrap tightly in plastic wrap or parchment paper and keep refrigerated until ready to use.

Addison, The Grand Del Mar's Butter-Baked King Crab with Green Apple and Pistachio Couscous

By Chef William Bradley

Four king crab legs (about 4 ounces each)
1/2 cup (8 tablespoons) French butter, softened
2 cups couscous
1 cup chicken stock
4 tablespoons pistachio oil
1 cup diced green apple
Sea salt to taste

Preheat oven to 350 degrees Fahrenheit.

Remove the crab leg meat by cracking the shell in half and carefully pull the meat out. Place on a baking sheet and set aside.

Pour couscous on a separate baking sheet and place in oven for approximately 5 minutes to toast. While couscous is toasting, heat the chicken stock in a saucepot over medium heat and bring to a boil. Remove couscous from oven and pour into a bowl. Cover couscous with hot chicken stock and cover with plastic wrap. Allow couscous to steam for 5 minutes. Remove plastic wrap and season with pistachio oil, green apples and sea salt to taste. Toss until all ingredients are blended.

Adjust oven temperature to 325 degrees Fahrenheit. Spread 2 tablespoons of the softened butter onto each of the four crab legs and place in oven for 3 minutes.

To serve, spoon some couscous on each plate, and then place crab legs on top of couscous. Serve immediately. Serves 4.

Witch Creek Winery's House Recipe French Beef Stew

Serve with their "Old Vine" Zinfandel

1 lb quality stew meat
1 tablespoon olive oil
1 large chopped brown onion
1 cup mushrooms
1 cup tomatoes (chopped)
2 cloves garlic
1/2 bottle of red wine
1 tablespoon Italian seasonings
1 bay leaf
Dash of salt and pepper

Brown the meat in the olive oil. Turn down the heat to a simmer and add the onion, garlic, mushrooms, tomatoes and red wine. Season with salt and pepper, Italian seasonings and bay leaf. Cover and simmer for 2–4 hours until tender. Serve with plain pasta or rice and steamed vegetables

Witch Creek House Recipe

You may want to serve this dish with one of their Rhône blends such as "La Mariage." The winery suggests accompanying the pork with plain rice and a vegetable.

Roast Pork Loin with Mushroom Sauce

1 boneless or boned pork loin
1 cup cream sherry
1/2 cup minced red onions
4 tablespoon butter
1 cup fresh, diced mushrooms
1/2 cup port
1 handful fresh cilantro

Roast the pork loin. Deglaze the roasting pan with the cream sherry. In a sauce pan, sauté the red onions in the butter. Add the mushrooms, the port and the mixture from the deglazed pork pan. Cover the pan and adjust the heat to medium-high. This will cook the mushrooms quickly. Once the mushrooms are tender but have retained their shape, remove the lid and turn the heat to high. The mixture will reduce and thicken in about 5 minutes. Make sure you watch and stir the ingredients. Once the mixture has thickened, add the cilantro and immediately serve over the pork loin.

Callaway's Grilled Baby Lamb Chops with Red Wine Glaze

Chef Michael Henry of Meritage at Callaway

It pairs very nicely with Callaway's 2005 Winemaker's Reserve Cabernet Franc or more boldly with the 2004 Winemaker's Reserve Meritage.

Note:

This is a fairly simple dish that requires three things, marinating the lamb, reducing the sauce to a glaze and cooking the lamb to your liking.

Lamb Chops, cap removed, cleaned
Minced garlic
Rosemary, thyme and marjoram, chopped
Olive oil
Kosher salt and black pepper
12 oz red wine, dry
Shallots, slivered
1 oz sugar
2 oz butter

1. Marinate lamb chops with garlic, herbs, olive oil and salt and pepper. Lamb can be marinated up to a day in advance, or longer if you omit the salt.

2. Prepare your grill, good and hot, with the grates cleaned and oiled.

3. While the grill is heating up, briefly sauté the shallots, sugar and butter. When the shallots are caramelized, deglaze the pan with the red wine and reduce until it becomes syrup. Set aside.

4. Grill the lamb chops to your liking, about 2-3 minutes on each side for medium or pink.

5. Serve immediately with the glaze; eating with your fingers is ok.

Wine & Sulfites

My facialist once told me that the sulfites in wine and cheese weren't good for my skin. Because I was relaxed, I didn't want to get into a discussion about how I was a wine writer and needed to drink wine and partake in cheese. Since she said that sulfites were the culprit, I made a mission out of finding out if there were any wines available without sulfites. Unfortunately, they weren't easy to find and as I delved into research on the issue I found that sulfites were getting a bad rap.

According to articles on the website www.wine intro.com written by Lisa Shea, all wines naturally have sulfites in them because it's a compound that nature puts in growing plants to prevent microbial growth. Thus, sulfites are in foods like grapes, onions and garlic. She goes on to mention that most winemakers add more sulfites to wine so the wine will last longer but there are some wines made that just include natural sulfites. These are wines that will only last about 18 months and are meant to be drunk young. Since many wines are meant to age, it seems natural that the sulfites would be added by a winery so a wine could sit in the bottle for a while.

The online articles mention a few other culprits that may cause reactions in people while drinking wine. Sometimes tannins in wine have caused mild to severe headaches in people but again, these are naturally occurring compounds and have been purported as being good antioxidants. Think about all the healthy hype tea gets. The article goes on to say that some people who are sensitive to their serotonin levels may have a problem with tannins because they "bind starches while being digested" and the starches are what the body uses to produce serotonin and thus it sometimes starves the body of the starches it needs.

Still another article on the same site mentions that cogeners might be a problem for people. According to the article, cogeners are contaminants found in low quality wine. One known cogener is methanol which my handy dictionary on my MacBook Pro describes as a "toxic, colorless, volatile flammable liquid alcohol originally made by distillation from wood and now chiefly by oxidizing methane."

Finally, another section on the site mentions the histamines in wines might cause reactions in some people. It says it's sometimes blamed when a wine drinker gets flushed while drinking. Again, however, it appears that the histamines are a natural substance that can also be found in foods like fish, chocolate and cheese. Aha, there's that cheese reference again. Perhaps it's not the sulfites I'm reacting to but rather the histamines. If that were the case, though, it would be better for me to drink white wines because according to the article they have less histamines than reds. Darn, I prefer reds!

Still more research on sulfites in wine seems to point to the fact that people might be blaming them for their troubles unfairly. On the www.ecowine.com website, it mentions that the FDA says only .4% of the population, translating into about a million people, are considered highly allergic to sulfites, and that the rest of the 99.75% of the population are at no risk. For the very small group of sulfite-sensitive people, the site suggests considering organic wines because most of them contain just minimal amounts of natural sulfites.

Andrew Waterhouse, a master student at UC Davis researching wine and headaches, writes on an online research paper (http://waterhouse.ucdavis.edu/winecomp/so2.htm) that sulfites are produced by the human body at 1000 milligrams per day and most wines average 80 milligrams per liter or 10 milligrams per glass of wine. He states the fact that whites have more sulfites than reds and that all wines contain some form of sulfites.

None of the research I found about sulfites mentions skin reactions. A few articles say that it could cause lung problems with asthmatics and that sulfites are sometimes blamed for headaches. So, in the final analysis it appears that most likely sulfites are not to be blamed for skin reactions. I've always lived by the motto "moderation in everything" and so I'll still be drinking wine in moderation and matching it with cheese.

San Diego County

San Diego has wineries in various parts of the county. The areas where the wineries are grouped are: Carlsbad, Central San Diego, Julian/Ramona, Rancho Bernardo/Escondido/San Marcos/Fallbrook and Warner Springs. You will probably want to make a separate trip to visit each grouped area.

There are quite a few wine grape growers that don't have tasting rooms so the wineries included here are ones that will let you visit either their vineyard, tasting room or both. Some wineries are open by appointment only. It's a good idea to check with the wineries you plan on visiting before you head out to make sure they'll be open.

In January, 2006 the Ramona area was successful at securing a Ramona American Viticultural Area (AVA). San Pasqual Valley (Escondido area) also enjoys AVA status acquired in years past. Wineries are sprouting up almost every day so be on the lookout for even more wineries in the future. Zoning laws have eased up to make it easier for wineries to open up. However, it's not as easy to open up a tasting room. Wineries that are forming in the area include Accidental Winery, Arroyo Dulce Cellars, Broquer Vineyards, Cactus Star Vineyard, Carlsbad Coastal Winery, Carson Vineyard, Century Tubes, Chuparosa Vineyards, Adobe Vineyard, Amarillo Road Vineyard, Chateau Viognier, Chinnok Cellars Vineyards, Dube Vineyards, Eagle Gap Vineyards, Hellanback Ranch Vineyard, Mahogany Mountain, Mais Fica Winery, Edwards Vineyard and Cellars, Kohill Winery, Orangewood Winery, Pyramid Winery, Woof'n Rose Vineyard, Paccielo Vineyard, Rancho del Fuego, Red Horse Winery and Epicurean Shop, Samuel Givens Winery, Walter Best Winery and Trefol Vineyard.

Lodging - Pampering

GRAND DEL MAR RESORT

www.thegranddelmar.com
5300 Grand Del Mar Court, San Diego, CA 92130
(858) 314-2000

The resort that houses the awarding winning Addison restaurant is like one you might find in Italy. Large lawns and water fountains grace the outside and indoors you'll find details like marble floors, imported stone and handpainted ceilings. The hotel along with the spa and golf course have all won top awards and it's only about five miles from the beach.

Wine Event

SAN DIEGO BAY WINE & FOOD FESTIVAL

www.worldofwineevents.com
858-578-9463

An almost week long extravaganza of wine tastings, cooking classes and events all culminating in a final, eye popping day of more food and wine than you could ever consume in one day. The festival occurs in November at the downtown Embarcadero.

Carlsbad

On a clear day you can see almost anything. That might be the best way to describe Carlsbad. East of Interstate 5 you will find the Carlsbad Company Stores, where you can enjoy shopping and have lunch at Bellefleur Restaurant. Quaint shops line the boulevard by the sea to the west of I-5, and among those shops you'll find Witch Creek Winery.

Lodging ~ Hotels

FOUR SEASONS RESORT AVIARA
www.fourseasons.com/aviara
7100 Four Seasons Point
(760) 603-6800

A luxury stay, but worth it if you can afford it. Amenities at this 5-star hotel include a golf course, spa, tennis courts, volleyball, and four restaurants. Some rooms offer views of Batiquitos Lagoon.

CARLSBAD INN
www.carlsbadinn.com
3075 Carlsbad Boulevard
(800) 235-3939

Closer to the coast and the wineries. The inn is 100 yards from the beach and offers a pool, gym, game room, and sauna. Reasonable price for a beach location.

Rancho Bernardo/ Escondido San Marcos/Fallbrook

This area is marked with rolling hills between the sea and the desert. The area produces many avocados, citrus fruits and grapes. It was once a well-respected wine district but lost its distinction after Prohibition. Only now is it regaining its vineyards.

Lodging - Moderate

RANCHO BERNARDO INN
www.ranchobernardoinn.com
17550 Bernardo Oaks Drive, San Diego, CA 92128
(858) 675-8500

The inn is well known in the area for its golf course and restaurant. A stay includes a full breakfast at the Veranda Restaurant. The facilities include a golf course, spa, pools, Jacuzzis and tennis courts.

RANCHO BERNARDO HOLIDAY INN
www.holidayinn.com
17065 West Bernardo Drive, San Diego, CA 92127
(858) 485-6530

Close to the Bernardo Winery, this hotel offers a more affordable choice and is kid friendly.

Ramona/Warner Springs

Ramona is an area that many San Diegans drive through in order to get to Julian. However, there's more to the area than that. Ramona is recognized as an American Viticultural Area and has not only been growing grapes, but wine tasting rooms are sprouting up too.

Warner Springs is located north of Julian. Shadow Mountain Vineyards is just past Warner Springs (the drive from Santa Ysabel is about a half hour). So you can also drive here if you're heading to Julian.

Lodging - Resort

WARNER SPRINGS RANCH

www.warnersprings.com
31652 Highway 79, Warner Springs, CA 92086
(760) 782-4200

Warner Springs Ranch is a historic resort originally established in 1844. Cozy cottages with fireplaces and refrigerators without televisions or phones allow you to truly relax.

Lodging - Bed & Breakfast

EAGLES NEST WINERY & COTTAGE

www.eaglesnestwinery.com
18261 Chablis Road, Ramona, CA 92065
(760) 505-8229

Eagles Nest in Ramona is a cottage with a small boutique winery that has a couple of thousand grapevines planted along the property's hillside. Owned by Dennis and Julie Grimes, you'll have to either stay at the beautiful vacation cottage or book an appointment to taste their hand-made wines. They produce wine from grapes grown on the property as well as purchased grapes from the Ramona and South Coast Appellations. Some of the varieties you'll find here are Chardonnay, Cabernet Sauvignon, Cabernet Franc, Merlot, Syrah, Tempranillo, Viognier and Zinfandel.

Julian

To residents of San Diego, Julian is as American as apple pie. Ask any San Diegan about Julian and they're bound to talk about the apple pie. The most popular time of year in Julian is the fall during the apple harvest. (The town can get very crowded at that time but a glimpse of the colorful fall leaves may be encouragement enough to brave the crowds.) Tourists crowd the streets in summer as well.

Some people in the area don't necessarily like the crowds, but they welcome them because they are beginning to realize that tourists are what make the town run. Some locals are pursuing ways to add more parking areas, picnic tables, and restaurants to make the town more friendly to visitors.

Julian is surrounded by Volcan Mountain and the Cuyamaca Mountains. The community dates back to 1869 when gold was first discovered there. Today, you can still pan for gold at one of the booths along the town's center on Main Street.

The area's founding father was Drue Bailey, a former soldier. He, along with his brother, Frank Bailey, and cousins Webb and Mike Julian, were heading to Arizona when they stopped to rest in what is now the area of Julian. Drue liked the area so much that he and his companions ended up staying. Frank decided to continue to Arizona but returned in 1870 when he heard of the gold discovery. The town's name comes from Mike Julian, Bailey's cousin.

Julian's first apple orchards were planted in the 1870s by Thomas Brady. The demand for apple pie keeps apple growers busy; apple trees are everywhere in Julian. Almost no one leaves the area without trying a piece of apple pie or drinking some cider. Although Julian is most famous for its apples, the area has a little-known secret. It's called Menghini Winery and a trip to Julian wouldn't be complete without visiting this mom-and-pop delight.

Look for **Orfila Winery's** tasting room located at 4470 Highway 78, Julian, (760) 765-0102. Their website is www.orfila.com. Generally, you'll see it as you're driving into town if you take Highway 78. Also, **Witch Creek Winery** has a tasting room located in downtown Julian at 2000 Main Street, Suite 106 and 107. (760) 765-2023. www.witchcreek-winery.com.

Witch Creek in Julian is a place for tasting only. It opened in 1984, but you won't find vineyards here; their wines are brought from their Carlsbad winery of the same name.

Julian Chamber of Commerce
(760) 765-1857
www.julianca.com

Lodging ~ Bed and Breakfasts

ORCHARD HILL COUNTRY INN
www.orchardhill.com
2502 Washington Street, Julian California 92036
(760) 765-1700

A lovely four diamond bed & breakfast close to downtown Julian. You will feel embraced by the warm, inviting atmosphere of the rooms and staff. The romantic setting attracts people celebrating anniversaries and birthdays. Recognized by *Sunset Magazine* as "one of the top six lodges in the west."

JULIAN BED AND BREAKFAST GUILD
(760) 765-1555

This guild is a network of bed and breakfast providers. They offer a directory with information about each participating property. All guild members are listed with the Automobile Club (AAA). Call for rates.

Directions to Julian

From San Diego take I-8 east or Highway 78 east to Highway 79. The main town of Julian is located on Highway 79 (about a 90-minute drive from San Diego).

San Diego Wine Bars

Wine Bars are becoming so popular now that most San Diegan's practically have one within walking distance of their home or office. So, this list focuses on wine bars that have been around for a while or are a unique experience. I love the small neighborhood wine bars but to list them here might crowd their already sometimes over-crowded rooms.

DECANTER WINE LOUNGE AND RESTAURANT
www.decanterwinelounge.com
18021 Calle Ambiente, Rancho Santa Fe, CA 92067
(858) 756-9333

A new wine bar and restaurant offering 200 wines by the glass and seasonal cuisine. Located in the European style shopping center of the upscale Cielo Village. Classy and chic environment.

ENO WINE BAR
www.enowinerooms.com
1500 Orange Avenue, Coronado, CA 92118
(619) 522-8546

Eno is an upscale wine tasting room at the Hotel Del Coronado. Offers Eno-versity classes focusing on both novice and expert wine connoisseurs.

THE GRAPE
www.thegrapebar.com
823 Fifth Avenue, San Diego (Gaslamp Quarter)
(619) 238-8010

One of the original wine bars in San Diego. The wine tasting atmosphere is achieved by the use of wine barrels as tables and an ivy-covered entrance. The wine menu is extensive. The Grape offers wines by the glass as well as flights of three tastes of wine, and most are of different varietals.

SPLASH WINE LOUNGE

www.asplashofwine.com
3043 University Avenue, San Diego, CA 92104
(619) 296-0714

A new wine bar reminiscent of the one I experienced in the Chianti region in Italy. The bar features an Italian technology system that allows tasters to try one ounce pours (splash).

TANGO WINE COMPANY

www.tangowine.com
2161 India Street, San Diego CA 92101
(619) 564-7700

Offers unique events like blind tasting workshops, wine dinners and Wine N' Writer's featuring popular writers appearances.

THE WINE LOVER

www.thewinelover.us
3968 Fifth Avenue, Hillcrest
(619) 294-9200

Another original San Diego wine bar, The Wine Lover has mood lighting and is centered around a curved bar in the middle. It's small, so you have to squeeze by the bar to get to the back tables, but it's worth it. The bar has a sophisticated tone. The bartenders are friendly and there's a long list of wines available.

THE 3RD CORNER

www.the3rdcorner.com
Ocean Beach: 2265 Bacon Street, San Diego, CA 92107
(619) 223-2700

Encinitas: 897 S. Coast Highway, Ste. F 104, Encinitas, CA 92024
(760) 942-2104

The 3rd Corner ushered in the new wine bar era in San Diego when it opened in Ocean Beach. Finally, there was an inviting place to go just to have a drink and meet with friends that wouldn't throw you out by 11 p.m. Just don't fall asleep on their couches. A big no-no.

WINE STEALS

www.winestealssd.com

Hillcrest: 1243 University Avenue, San Diego, CA 92103
(619) 295-1188

Point Loma: 2970 Truxtun Road, San Diego, CA 92106
(619) 221-1959

Cardiff: 1953 San Elijo Avenue, Cardiff by the Sea, CA 92007
(760) 230-2657

As the name implies, Wine Steals offers wines by the glass that won't break the bank and in unique environments. Each location offers a different setting – all inspired by traditional European wineries.

San Diego Wine Focused Restaurants
Wine Spectator Grand Award Winner

WINESELLAR & BRASSERIE
www.winesellar.com
9550 Waples Street, Suite 115
San Diego, CA 92121
(858) 450-9557

Before the wine trend even got started and most people even knew what the Wine Spectator was, The WineSellar & Brasserie was turning out inspired food at their upstairs, romantically-lit restaurant and selling sommelier chosen wine at their downstairs wine shop. Year after year, Wine Spectator gives them their highest award. What more is there to say? Oh, make sure you get directions, they're hidden among office buildings.

Top Picks of Wine Spectator's Best of Award of Excellence restaurants

ADDISON AT THE GRAND DEL MAR RESORT
www.addisondelmar.com
5200 Grand Del Mar Way, San Diego, CA 92130
(858) 314-1900

Words are hard to describe the experience you'll have at Addison located at the Grand Del Mar Resort. Addison is the only five star and five diamond restaurant in Southern California. The luxurious setting makes you feel you've flown thousands of miles to get there, and the buttoned-up service is impeccable. The young wine director, Jesse Rodriguez, knows his stuff and has been recognized locally as the Best Sommelier by Ranch & Coast Magazine along with others. The California Restaurant Association, 2008 recognized Addison as having the best California Wine List. Offerings include a chef recommended seven-course wine and food pairing down to a four-course experience.

BARREL ROOM (RANCHO BERNARDO)

www.thebarrelroomsandiego.com
16765 Bernardo Center Drive, San Diego, CA 92128
(858) 673-7512

The Barrel Room wine bar and restaurant was started out of a love for the wine industry. Grant Tondro didn't set out to open a wine focused restaurant when he began his career working at Von's at the age of 16. Today Grant, his friend Zach and brother Nate join together to run the restaurant. Grant describes his restaurant as a place that offers a big selection of wines for retail purchases, a large selection of wines by the glass and a full restaurant section.

Unique Wine Restaurants

WINE VAULT & BISTRO

www.winevaultbistro.com
3731-A India Street, San Diego CA 92103
(619) 295-3939

The Wine Vault & Bistro specializes in wine and food pairings and is located in a somewhat hidden location above popular Saffron restaurant and Gelato Vero Cafe near Washington Street. The husband and wife team owners create a friendly environment with shared tables and purposely sitting people with one another to create interactions. They focus on affordable wine paired dinners. They use local produce to create their dishes

BELLEFLEUR RESTAURANT

www.bellefleur.com
610 Paseo del Norte, Carlsbad, California 92008
(760) 603-1919

Bellefleur Restaurant is located near the Carlsbad Flower Fields, a 50-acre ranunculus field that blooms magnificently in spring. They have their own wines made by Rutherford Winery in Paso Robles. You'll find Chardonnay, Cabernet and Merlot Bellefleur wine.

San Diego Specialty Wine Retailers

HOLIDAY WINE CELLAR
www.holidaywinecellar.com
302 West Mission Avenue, Escondido, CA 92025
(760) 745-1200

This shop has a wine cellar and sells rare and vintage finds.

NORTH COUNTY WINE COMPANY
www.northcountywinecompany.com
1099 San Marcos Boulevard, San Marcos, CA 92078
(760) 744-2119

A retail shop with a tasting bar featuring unique choices as well as a large selection of wines at good prices. Unique and inviting environment.

SAN DIEGO WINE & CULINARY CENTER
www.sdwineculinary.com
200 Harbor Drive, Suite 120, San Diego, CA 92101
(619) 231-6400

The downtown location offers locally produced wines at a tasting bar, a retail shop, food and wine classes and more.

SAN DIEGO WINE COMPANY
www.sandiegowine.net
7080 Miramar Road, Ste. 100, San Diego, CA 92121
(858) 586-WINE (9463) (800) 650-WINE (9463)
Offers discount wines from around the world.

VINTAGE WINES, LTD.
www.vintagewinessd.com
6904 Miramar Road , San Diego, CA 92121
(858) 549-2112

Well known for its Zinfandels, this shop has a wine bar and carries high-quality wines. Wine classes are also offered here.

WINE BANK
www.sdwinebank.com
363 Fifth Avenue, Suite 100, San Diego, CA 92101
(619) 234-7487

Sells wines at discount prices.

THE WINE CONNECTION
www.thewineconnection.com
2650 Via De La Valle, C-130, Del Mar, CA 92014
(858) 350-9292

Offers domestic and imported wines.

WINE STREET
www.winestreet.com
6986 El Camino Real, Carlsbad, CA 92009
(760) 431-8455

A North County shop with a nice selection (it also holds wine tastings).

Where To Buy Items
For A Picnic Basket

BREAD & CIE

www.breadandciecatering.com
350 University Avenue, San Diego, CA 92103
(619) 683-9322

Bread & Cie makes bread with age-old artisan breadmaking techniques like ones you'd find in Europe. You can find the locally made bread at many stores throughout the area, but a trip to the Hillcrest shop engulfs you with an array of choices like black olive, fig and anise, three raison, sourdough and more.

THE LINKERY

www.thelinkery.com
3794 30th Street, San Diego, CA 92104
(619) 255-8778

The Linkery is a restaurant and to-go deli that offers meats that are secured from independent farmers and co-ops offering grass fed meats and who consider traditional sustainable methods. Buy their hand made sausages and breads for your basket.

VENISSIMO CHEESE

www.venissimo.com
San Diego: 754 W Washington Street, San Diego, CA 92103
(619) 491-0708

Del Mar: 2710 Via de la Valle, Del Mar, CA 92104
(858) 847-9616

The ultimate collection of cheese varieties is here. They've carried over 1,200 varieties of cheeses since they've been open and if they don't have what you want they'll order it for you to arrive the next day.

EXTRAORDINARY DESSERTS

www.extraordinarydesserts.com

1430 Union Street, San Diego, CA 92101 (619) 294-7001

2929 Fifth Avenue, San Diego, CA 92103 (619) 294-2132

A long running dessert hot spot, the environment and quality desserts will bring you back again and again. Lavender shortbread, petit lemon cupcakes, lemon meringue pie and apple brie scones are just some of the offerings.

CHUAO CHOCOLATIER

www.chuaochocolatier.com

There are chocolate cafes at:

937 S. Coast Highway 101, Suite C-109, Encinitas, CA 92024 (760) 635-1444

3485 Del Mar Heights Road, Suite A-1, Del Mar, CA 92130 (858) 755-0770

4465 La Jolla Village Drive H-09, University Town Centre, SD, CA 92122

(858) 546-1463

Chuao offers handcrafted chocolates made with Belgian and French techniques in unexpected flavors like Earl Grey chocolate bars and caramel fudge chipotle truffles. They even have wine and chocolate pairings available.

San Diego Wineries

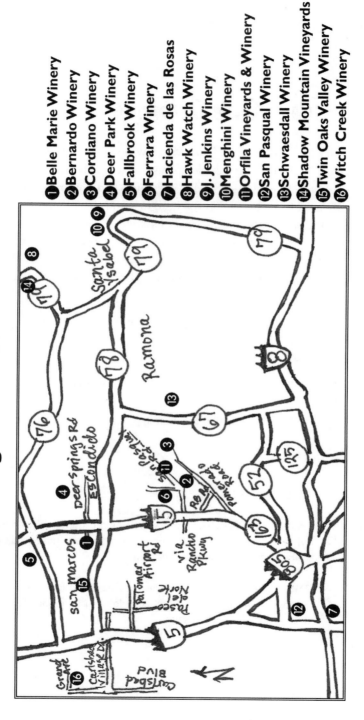

1. Belle Marie Winery
2. Bernardo Winery
3. Cordiano Winery
4. Deer Park Winery
5. Fallbrook Winery
6. Ferrara Winery
7. Hacienda de las Rosas
8. Hawk Watch Winery
9. J. Jenkins Winery
10. Menghini Winery
11. Orfila Vineyards & Winery
12. San Pasqual Winery
13. Schwaesdall Winery
14. Shadow Mountain Vineyards
15. Twin Oaks Valley Winery
16. Witch Creek Winery

Belle Marie Winery

It's hard not to miss Belle Marie Winery from the I-15 freeway. Their Chateau Dragoo castle sits high on a hill above.

A walk through their garden with citrus and fruit trees puts you in a relaxed frame of mind as you head to the tasting room.

This winery brings their grapes from vineyards they own in Guadalupe Valley in Baja California and makes more than 30 different wines every year. You'll find varieties like Grenache, Malbec, Petite Sirah, Late Harvest Primitivo and Chateauneu du Pape.

 LOCATION: 26312 Mesa Rock Road (near the Deer Springs Road exit off I-15) Escondido, California 92026
(760) 796-7557

 WEBSITE: www.bellemarie.com/index.html

 HOURS: 11 a.m. to 5 p.m. daily

 TOURS: By appointment

 TASTING CHARGE: Yes

 WINE FOCUS: The winery focuses on "Meritage" wines: wines with a mixture of grape varieties, for example a mix of Cabernet Sauvignon and Nebbiollo.

 DIRECTIONS: Take I-15 toward Escondido and exit at Deer Springs Road, heading west. Make a left at Mesa Rock Road. The winery is on the right.

Bernardo Winery

Bernardo Winery's rustic setting is surrounded by antiques and is in the middle of a residential area. It's one of the oldest regularly operating wineries in Southern California established in 1889. In 1928 the Rizzo family bought it. Ross Rizzo took over in 1962 from his father, Vincent Rizzo.

The first thing you'll notice when you arrive are the specialty shops lining a path toward the tasting room. The shops are open from 10 a.m. to 5 p.m. Tuesday through Sunday. They have a park and picnic area and banquet and party facilities. There's also a farmer's market on Fridays from 9 a.m. to noon. The winery imports their grapes from various parts of California. Some of the unique wines you'll find are Pinot Grigio, French Colombard, Chablis, Burgundy, Carignane and Concord.

LOCATION: 13330 Paseo del Verano Norte, San Diego, California 92128 (858) 487-1866

WEBSITE: www.bernardowinery.com

HOURS: 9 a.m. to 5 p.m. daily

TOURS: Yes but private tours only

TASTING CHARGE: Yes

WINE FOCUS: Reds

DIRECTIONS: Take I-15 toward Rancho Bernardo to the Rancho Bernardo Road turnoff. Head east and make a left at Pomerado Road. At Paseo Del Verano Norte make a right. From there, the winery is 1.5 miles on the right.

Cordiano Winery

Owned by Rosa and Gerado Cordiano, Cordiano Winery is a small boutique winery. According to Rosa "people love the family atmosphere and gorgeous views of San Pasqual Valley." They offer food ahead of time if you let them know you're coming. The couple are originally from South Italy. They bought 20 acres of avocado groves and cut 2200 trees down to make room for Cabernet Sauvignon, Tempranillo, Cabernet Franc, Merlot, Syrah and Zinfandel grapes. White wine grapes didn't grow well at their vineyard so they buy Chardonnay grapes from Paso Robles. This is a small production winery. The first wines were produced in 2002.

 LOCATION: 15732 Highland Valley Road, Escondido, CA 92025 (760) 480-6673

 WEBSITE: www.cordianowinery.com

 HOURS: 11 a.m. to sunset Wednesday through Sunday, Monday and Tuesday by reservation only

 TOURS: Yes

 TASTING CHARGE: Yes

 WINE FOCUS: Cabernet Sauvignon

 DIRECTIONS: Take I-15 and exit at Pomerado Road head East and take Highland Valley Road East. Winery is about five miles from the bottom of the hill.

Deer Park Winery & Auto Museum

Deer Park Winery is located on 15 acres in the Escondido hills. Deer Park's wines are produced in Escondido as well as at their sister winery in Napa Valley, which was established in 1891. The grounds are part of what makes a trip to this winery worthwhile. There's a creek bed with a foot bridge surrounded by a green lawn that looks like it's just begging for a bride and groom to be photographed there (wedding and reception sites are available).

Or, if you enjoy classic cars, you'll also want to make sure you visit this winery. There's a museum that features more than 100 classic automobiles.

The winery has picnic tables on the grounds; there's also an on-site deli, gift shop, market and wine afficionado shop.

 LOCATION: 29013 Champagne Boulevard, Escondido, California 92026 (760) 749-1666

 WEBSITE: www.deerparkwinery.com

 HOURS: Call beforehand, open at inconsistent times

TOURS: No

 TASTING CHARGE: Call for more information

 WINE FOCUS: Distinctive, full bodied wine

DIRECTIONS: Take I-15 to the Deer Springs/Mountain Meadow exit. Head east 1 block to Champagne Boulevard. Make a left. Deer Park Winery & Auto Museum is 3 miles north on the right.

Fallbrook Winery

Ted Gourvitz, owner of Fallbrook Winery, purchased the winery property in the 1980s and replanted grape vines on 20 of the 36 acres. You'll find varieties like Cabernet Sauvignon, Merlot, Syrah, Petite Verdot and Cabernet Franc. The remaining acres are filled with avocado and lemon trees. You can visit the winery in Fallbrook or go to their downtown tasting room, Fallbrook Winery Cellar, right next to the San Diego Wine and Culinary Center. Some of their wines that have recently won awards are a gold for the '08 Sauvignon Blanc from the '09 San Diego International Wine Competition and a platinum (better than gold) for the '06 Sauvignon Blanc ('07 Critic's Challenge International Wine Competition). The winery is part of the South Coast appellation but is also in the process of applying for Fallbrook appellation status. You can find their wines in San Diego stores and restaurants in addition to the winery.

 LOCATION: 2554 Via Rancheros, Fallbrook, California, 92028 (760) 728-0156

 WEBSITE: www.fallbrookwinery.com

 HOURS: Monday through Friday 10 to 5 p.m. By appointment on the weekends

 TOURS: Yes, by appointment

 **TASTING CHARGE:** Yes

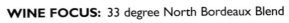 **WINE FOCUS:** 33 degree North Bordeaux Blend

 DIRECTIONS: Take I-15 toward Fallbrook and exit at 76-West. Turn right at Mission Road and another right at Green Canyon Road. Then right at Winterhaven. Then it's a left on Via Arroyo and another left at Via Ranceros. Winery is on left.

Ferrara Winery

Ferrara Winery is a state historical point of interest (designated in 1971). The winery has been producing wine since 1932 and was started by George Ferrara. Today, you'll find a tasting room that hasn't changed much since the winery's beginnings. It's a good place to feel what it might have been like back in the early days. They have unique wines here like Generation III Port, Nectar De Luz, Bella Serena, Chardo-Cat, Muscat Alexandria, Vino Rosso and Carignana/Rouge. They even sell different grape variety fruit juices.

 LOCATION: 1120 West 15th Avenue, Escondido, California 92025 (760) 745-7632

 WEBSITE: www.ferrarawinery.com

 HOURS: 10 a.m. to 5 p.m. daily. Closed on Thanksgiving, Christmas, New Year's Day and Easter

 TOURS: No

 TASTING CHARGE: No

 WINE FOCUS: Dry, medium dry and dessert wines

 DIRECTIONS: Take I-15 toward Escondido to Ninth Avenue and head east to Upas Avenue. Make a right and drive south to 15th Avenue. Make a right. (The entrance looks like a residential driveway, but there are numerous signs to help guide you.)

Hacienda de las Rosas

In 1860s cowboy garb Tammy Rimes and William Holzhauer, owners of Hacienda de las Rosas, greet customers at their Old Town tasting room. Although their winery is located in Ramona where they grow mostly Tempranillo and mission grapes, they say they'd rather "go where people are." That statement fits the couple who are there to please the guests at the tasting room. William's jokes and Tammy's sweet demeanor will keep you around tasting their selection of red and white wines. Try their unique wine varieties like Tempranillo, Petite Sirah and Sauvignon Blanc. The winery focuses on Spanish wine-making traditions modeled after the California missions and they combine their love of their Peruvian Paso horses with the family motto of drink fine wine, ride fine horses.

 TASTING ROOM LOCATION: Fiesta de Reyes Plaza del Pasado, Old Town, 2754 Calhoun Street, San Diego 92110 (619) 840-5579

 WEBSITE: www.haciendawinery.com

 HOURS: 11:30 a.m to 7 p.m. Monday through Thursday, 11:30 a.m. to 9 p.m. Friday to Saturday

 TOURS: Special "Wine and Spirits" walking tour of Old Town followed by wine tasting

 TASTING CHARGE: Yes

 WINE FOCUS: Wines made from locally grown San Diego grapes

 DIRECTIONS: From San Diego take the I-8 freeway to the Taylor street exit and head South. At Juan Street make a left. Enter at the Juan Street entrance.

Hawk Watch Winery

Hawk Watch Winery is a small production "micro-boutique" winery in Warner Springs producing 600 cases a year. Mike Schnell, part owner, came up with the micro-boutique phrase himself to describe a winery where "you have a true sense that this is the owner's passion." Hawk Watch is owned by Mike and Lisa Schnell who maintain full time jobs in addition to operating the vineyard, winery and tasting room. Mike's full time job is the assistant winemaker at Leonesse Cellars and Temecula Valley Winery Management.

The couple purchased 10 acres in Sunshine Summit in 2002 and have spent years creating a sense of true ownership in their winery and vineyard by doing the work themselves. They cleared the property of brush and trees and then planted 3,800 grapevines and hand-crafted their trellising.

They specialize in Syrah and Rhone blends, but also produce Sauvignon Blanc, Meritage, Grenache, Dry Orange Muscat, Zinfandel and Muscat Canelli. The high altitude vineyards (over 3,200 feet in elevation) produce fruit with deep, intense color, flavor and complexity. Their 2005 Syrah won a Gold and two Silver medals in their first year of operation.

LOCATION: 27054 Chihuahua Valley Road, Warner Springs, CA 92086 (951) 326-4692

WEBSITE: www.hawkwatchwinery.com

HOURS: 10 a.m. to 5 p.m. Saturday and Sunday

TOURS: No, but the owners are open to answer questions

TASTING CHARGE: Yes

WINE FOCUS: Premium award winning reds, specifically Syrah.

DIRECTIONS: Take Highway 79 from Temecula or San Diego. At Chihuahua Valley Road head East.

J. Jenkins Winery

Jim and Jeanne Jenkins own J. Jenkins Winery located near the downtown area of Julian. The winery sits on 10 acres. Jim had wanted a winery for 30 years and while he was practicing medicine he used to go to Julian on the weekends to visit his friends, the Menghinis. He fell in love with the valley and so decided to purchase some property. They grow a number of varieties like Pinot Grigio and Pinot Noir. They make a unique wine called Dolcezza made up of 100% estate grown apples. Some of the other wines they produce are Viognier, Pinot Grigio, Syrah, Pinot Gris, Sauvignon Blanc and Cabernet Sauvignon. Visit their new wine production building and tasting room.

 LOCATION: 1255 Julian Orchards Drive, P.O. Box 2094 Julian, California 92036 (760) 765-3267

 WEBSITE: www.jenkinswinery.com

 HOURS: Saturday and Sunday, from 11 a.m. to 5 p.m.

 TOURS: Yes, by appointment

 TASTING CHARGE: Yes

 WINE FOCUS: Niche market wines that others aren't producing, like their Nouveau

 DIRECTIONS: From Highway 79 in Julian continue on Highway 79 headed north. After you leave Main Street the highway turns into Farmers Road. Make a left at Julian Orchards Drive.

Menghini Winery

When you arrive at the winery, you'll find the plants surrounding it are mostly apple trees although they do have a six acre vineyard. The inviting atmosphere of the tasting room is often accentuated by lounging dogs. The winey is owned by a husband and wife team, Michael and Toni Menghini, who produce 4,000 cases of wine each year.

Located just a few miles from downtown Julian, they have various events throughout the year like a Spring barrel tasting, grape stomp and art and music festival. They have a picnic area with tables for seasonal use.

Some of the wines you'll find here are Syrah, Sauvignon Blanc, Riesling and Cabernet Sauvignon.

 LOCATION: 1150 Julian Orchards Drive, Julian, California 92036 (760) 765-2072

 WEBSITE: www.menghiniwinery.com

 HOURS: 10 a.m. to 4 p.m. weekdays and 10 a.m. to 5 p.m. weekends.

 TOURS: Yes, by appointment

 TASTING CHARGE: Yes

 WINE FOCUS: Premium varietals

 DIRECTIONS: From Highway 79 in Julian continue on Highway 79 headed north. After you leave Main Street the highway turns into Farmers Road. Make a left at Julian Orchards Drive.

ORFILA VINEYARDS & WINERY

- Tasting Room
- Gift Shop
- Private Tastings
- Corporate Events
- Weddings
- Private Wine Labels
- Custom Etched & Hand-Painted Wine Bottles
- Free Guided Tours 2 pm Daily
- Orfila Wines & Gourmet Products Sold Online at **www.ORFILA.com**
- Look for the free tasting coupon in this book!

Love Wine? Join the Club!

ORFILA
W I N E
LOVERS

Call 1.800.868.9463 or visit
www.orfila.com/wine-club
for more information on
wine club member benefits.

13455 San Pasqual Road, Escondido, CA 92025
Open daily 10-6 pm (760) 738.6500 x 22

And don't forget to visit our Julian location:
4470 Hwy. 78, Julian, CA 92036 Open daily 10-5 pm (760) 765.0102

Orfila Vineyards & Winery

Alejandro Orfila owns San Diego's largest winery that sits in the San Pasqual Valley appellation on 70 acres just across from the San Diego Wild Animal Park. The grounds feature a picnic area overlooking a nearby golf course and an area for weddings and events. Inside, you'll find a large tasting room with products like T-shirts, olive oil, French bread and cheese for sale.

They've won a large number of prestigious awards and aren't afraid to travel across the country to enter competitions. Recently, they won a Critics Platinum (better than a gold) from the '08 Critics Challenge International Wine competition for their '05 Ambassador's Reserve Merlot. Their '06 Gewurztraminer won a double Gold from the '08 El Dorado County Fair and in '02 at the Atlanta International Wine Summit they won Best U.S. Red wine for their '99 Syrah.

 LOCATION: 13455 San Pasqual Road, Escondido, California 92025 (760) 738-6500

 WEBSITE: www.orfila.com

 HOURS: Open 10 a.m. to 6 p.m. daily except New Year's Day, Easter, July 4th, Thanksgiving and Christmas

 TOURS: Yes, free 20-minute tours offered at 2 p.m. daily

 TASTING CHARGE: Yes

 WINE FOCUS: Rhone style wines

 DIRECTIONS: Take I-15 toward Escondido and exit Via Rancho Parkway. Head east until you reach San Pasqual Road. Make a right. The winery is on the right.

San Pasqual Winery

San Pasqual Winery was recently purchased by Mike and Linda McWilliams who had originally thought about opening a tasting bar, but found San Pasqual for sale and decided to take advantage of the opportunity to offer locally made wine. The winery location (no grapes grown here but the wine is made at the winery) is central to most San Diegans, near Pacific Beach. A unique wine they're offering is called PB Passion and is made from passion fruit, not grapes. Most of the wine is made from grapes purchased in the Guadalupe valley of Mexico. Some of the grape wines being offered are Grenache Blanc de Noir, Chardonnay, Sauvignon Blanc, Tempranillo, Cabernet Sauvignon and Syrah.

 LOCATION: 5151 Santa Fe Street, Suite H, San Diego, CA 92109 (858) 270-7550

 WEBSITE: www.sanpasqualwinery.com

 HOURS: 12 to 4 p.m. Saturdays or by appointment

 TOURS: Yes, you can see most of the winery from the tasting room

 TASTING CHARGE: Yes, but you get a credit toward wine purchase.

 WINE FOCUS: Riojas reds from Guadalupe Valley

 DIRECTIONS: Take I-5 to Grand/Garnet exit near Pacific Beach. At Damon Avenue head East to Santa Fe Street and make a left. Winery is about a mile from Damon and Santa Fe.

Schwaesdall Winery

John Schwaesdall owns this winery with a tasting room that was the first commercial straw-bale (the walls have straw inside, which is used for insulation) room in San Diego. He makes wine from the 4 1/2 acres of red and white grapes he grows on his 6-acre property. Ramona has been designated an AVA (Agricultural Viniculture Area), known as the Ramona Valley. Schwaesdall Winery has beautiful grounds ideal for picnics, special events and weddings. Schwaesdall says Ramona has the same climate as the Rhône Valley in France and parts of Italy and the Ramona Valley is known as the "Rhône Valley of California." Often, you will be greeted by John when you arrive at the winery.

 LOCATION: 17677 Rancho de Oro Road, Ramona, California 92065 (760) 789-7547

 WEBSITE: www.schwaesdallwinery.com

 HOURS: 10 a.m. to 6 p.m. weekends

 TOURS: No

 TASTING CHARGE: Yes

 WINE FOCUS: Hand Crafted Red Wines, White, Ruby and Tawny Ports

 DIRECTIONS: Take I-8 east or Highway 78 east to Highway 67. Take Highway 67 to Schwaesdall Winery which is located right off of Highway 67 at Rancho de Oro Road (on the right hand side heading east).

Shadow Mountain Vineyards

The entrance to Shadow Mountain Vineyards is marked by a beautiful sign (like those in Temecula or Napa Valley) and is located just off Highway 79. Owners Alex and Pam McGeary handle most of the operations with Alex tending the vineyards and Pamela producing the labels for the bottles.

The winery boasts 65-year-old vines. The vineyard consists of more than 30 acres of rolling hills, and the winery sells most of its wine through the tasting room.

Alex works with local Warner Springs High School students to teach them the winemaking process.

Recent awards include a Gold from the Grand Harvest-Sonoma and two Silvers from the San Diego International and L.A. International Jerry Mead for their meritage blend and four Silvers for their '05 Merlot from O.C. Grand Harvest, West Coast Competition and Temecula Wine Society Competitions. You can stay overnight at one of their cottages on the property.

 LOCATION: 34680 Highway 79, Warner Springs, California 92086 (760) 782-0778

 WEBSITE: www.shadowmountainvineyards.com

 HOURS: 10 a.m. to 5 p.m. Wednesday through Sunday and most holidays that fall on a Monday

 TOURS: Yes, by appointment

 TASTING CHARGE: Yes

 WINE FOCUS: Premium white and red varietal wines from grapes grown on the estate.

 DIRECTIONS: 23 miles north of Santa Ysabel, take Highway 79 north toward Warner Springs. The winery is located on Highway 79.

Twin Oaks Valley Winery

Twin Oaks was established in 2002 by Frank Bons and Jacob Kappeler. The joint owners create premium estate Syrahs and Cabernet Sauvignons. They established the winery because they wanted to integrate grape growing and winemaking in one facility. They are proud of using locally grown and produced grapes from the San Diego region and are very involved in the growing of the fruit themselves.

They have 8 acres of Cabernet and Syrah at the winery. You can taste the wine at their tasting room and if you want a tour of the winery make a reservation. They won a bronze medal for their '04 Viognier from the Temecula Valley Wine Competition.

 TASTING ROOM LOCATION: 735 East Mission Road, San Marcos, CA 92069 (760) 471-9192

 WINERY LOCATION: 1575 Mulberry Drive, San Marcos, California 92069 (760) 471-8985

 WEBSITE: None

 HOURS: 9 a.m. to 5 p.m. Tuesday through Saturday

 TOURS: Yes, by appointment

 TASTING CHARGE: Yes

WINE FOCUS: Cabernet Sauvignon and Syrah

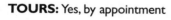 **DIRECTIONS:** Take I-15 or I-5 toward San Marcos and take the 78 west from the I-15 or east from the I-5. Get off on Twin Oaks headed north and make a right on East Mission Road.

Witch Creek Winery

Witch Creek Winery is close to Carlsbad Village, which has restaurants and antique stores on almost every corner.

The winery purchases grapes from various places throughout Southern California; oak barrels are stacked everywhere in the warehouse-like room. Witch Creek Winery opened in 1993 but there are no acres of vines here. According to Dave Wodehouse, the owner, their tour-de-force is their large variety of red wines. Their '06 Nebbiolo won Best of Class in the '09 San Francisco Wine Chronicle and their '06 Aglianico won a bronze medal at the SF Chronicle Wine Competition. Other unique varieties you'll find here are Tempranillo, Eye of Newt, Montepulciano, Mourvedre and Sauvignon Blanc

 LOCATION: 2906 Carlsbad Boulevard, Carlsbad, California 92008 (760) 720-7499

 WEBSITE: www.witchcreekwinery.com

 HOURS: 11 a.m. to 5 p.m. daily

 TOURS: Yes, by appointment

 TASTING CHARGE: Yes

 WINE FOCUS: Red wines

 DIRECTIONS: Take I-5 toward Carlsbad to Carlsbad Village Drive. Head west. Make a right on Carlsbad Boulevard/Coast Highway. The winery is located on the corner of Grand Avenue and Carlsbad Boulevard on the right.

San Diego wineries offering wholesale
and by appointment tastings.
Please call to make an appointment to visit them.

Gloriosa Vineyards, Campo

www.gloriosavineyards.com

Mert Thomas owns this winery. He planted vines on 40 acres 10 years
ago just three miles from the Mexican border and began selling wine
in 2008. To visit you will have to commit to purchase a case of wine.
They produce Syrah, Cabernet Sauvignon and Zinfandel. Wines are
available in some Albertsons in San Diego. Call for an appointment
and directions (619) 606-4112, (619) 589-9125 (619) 473-8566.

La Serenissima Vineyard

www.vinotiso.com

La Serenissima Vineyard was established in 1998 and was founded by
Dr. John Tiso. There are 16 acres of vines on the property and the
winery produces unique varieties like Cabernet Franc, Tempranillo
and Arneis. They limit their production to 800 cases and use
traditional Italian methods to produce the premium handcrafted
wines. By appointment only: 35168 Highway 79, Warner Springs, CA
92086 (760) 782-0644.

Lenora Winery

www.lenorawinery.com.

Lenora Winery showcases wines from small vineyards in the Ramona
AVA. You'll find wines like Sauvignon Blanc, Cabernet Sauvignon,
Grenache, Merlot, Sangiovese, Muscat and Zinfandel. Call for an
appointment and address: (760) 788-1388.

Orrin Vineyards & Winery
www.orrinvineyards.com

Located in the Warner Springs area, Orrin Vineyards and Winery is a wholesale winery creating small lot, handcrafted wine with grapes grown on their 20-acre estate. They produce Syrah, Merlot, Viognier and Zinfandel. To visit call (760) 782-0480. 325288 Highway 79, Warner Springs, CA 92086.

Pamo Valley Winery
www.pamovalleyvineyards.com

Located in the Ramona area, Pamo Valley Winery produces hand-crafted, premium and award winning wines like Syrah, Cabernet Sauvignon, Merlot, Sangiovese and Petite Sirah. For more information, to make an appointment and for their address contact the winery at (760) 271-3090.

Rock Canyon Vineyards
www.rockcanyonvineyards.com

Located in the Alpine area, Rock Canyon Vineyards is available for tastings by appointment only. Call for an appointment and address (760) 271-3090.

Salerno Winery
www.salernowinery.com

A boutique winery in Ramona that is in a historic adobe ranch house. Herman Salerno owns the winery and has been making wine for about 18 years. They produce Petite Sirah, Elegante (a red blend), Cabernet Sauvignon and Imagination (a Barolo blend). Wines are handcrafted. Their Petite Sirah won a double gold medal from the '06 Florida State International Competition. Call for an appointment: (760) 788-7160 17948 Highway 67, Ramona, CA 92065.

Temecula

Temecula has become a prominent winery area. Beginning in the '80s, Temecula boasted more wineries than the Cucamonga district to the north. The first plantings of vineyards in Temecula began in the 1960s with the help of the University of California at Davis, currently a main center for wine science. Hart Winery, Cilurzo and Callaway wineries were some of the first in the area. By 1981 there were 3,000 acres of vineyards in Temecula. Now, there are 30 wineries and more keep sprouting up all the time. Temecula's climate is often compared to the Mediterranean. Grape vines are planted in a basin 23 miles from the Pacific Ocean. The area receives cool, damp sea air from the ocean breezes that flow in through an open space in the west hills. This opening cools the valley enough to grow wine grapes. At night, cool air also keeps the temperature under control. The convenience of irrigation water helps vines grow here as well.

Temecula started out growing Napa and Sonoma Valley grape varieties like Chardonnay. However, the winemakers in the area began to realize that it would be better to plant grapes that were more favorable to their climate, specifically, Italian grapes. This realization came after a pest called the sharpshooter began infesting the grape vines and the wineries had to take out a lot of their vines.

It was Hart and Mount Palomar wineries that first produced Sangiovese, a red grape from Chianti, Italy. Those initial results proved impressive and some of the wineries began winning awards for their Italian varietal wines. Other new varietals like Mourvèdre and Nebbiolo were introduced at more wineries. Later, Rhone style varieties like Syrah and Viognier were planted. Now, you'll find the wineries getting more experimental growing even more varietals like Tempranillo and Petite Sirah.

Initially, Rancho California Road was the main winery center. Now, as more wineries open their doors, surrounding areas are being developed. You'll find wineries bunched up on DePortola Road and on Calle Contento. This book covers wineries that have tasting rooms. There are some wineries that are creating wines but don't open their doors to the public. Also, there are plans for more wineries in the near future. Keep your eyes open for new ones beyond what's listed. Isn't it fun to find new ones you haven't tried before?

Currently, some of the top wine varieties in Temecula are Syrah, Viognier and Zinfandel. The wineries are working with sustainable wine growing methods and considering soil management, vineyard water management, water conservation and pest management. Wine growers are working with spacing the grape vines closer together than in the past. They're stressing the grapes vines with deficit irrigation and using fewer fertilizers and pesticides. You'll find most of the Temecula wine producers represented at Shop Temecula Wines. They have wines from producers that don't have tasting rooms. Look for Atwood Estate Vineyard, Manteca, Cowper Family Vineyards, Masia de Yabar, Winery/Celebration Cellars, Monte de Oro Vineyards & Winery, Olive View Vineyard & Winery, Peltzer Farms Vineyard & Winery, Plateau Vineyards, Santa Maria Cellars, Barret Bird's Santa Margarita Winery as well as wines from wineries with tasting rooms. www.shoptemeculawines.com.

Directions to Temecula

Take I-15 toward Temecula to the Rancho California Road exit. Head east on Rancho California Road. The wineries are approximately a 45-minute drive from San Diego and an hour and a half drive from Los Angeles.

After crossing Ynez you'll find a road sign welcoming you to the wine country. You'll see this about 4 miles east of the freeway.

> Tip: Contact an Auto Club office near you and ask them for a Temecula Winery package.

Lodging - Hotels
ON THE FRINGES OF THE WINE COUNTRY

BEST WESTERN COUNTRY INN

www.bestwestern.com

27706 Jefferson Avenue, Temecula, California 92590

(951) 676-7378 or (800) 528-1234

Offers a continental breakfast, heated outdoor swimming pool and sauna.

EMBASSY SUITES

www.embassysuites.com

29345 Rancho California Road, Temecula, California 92591

(951) 676-5656 or (800) EMBASSY

You can't miss this hotel. You'll see it as soon as you exit the freeway.

COMFORT INN

www.comfortinn.com

27338 Jefferson Avenue, Temecula, California 92590

(951) 296-3788 or (800) 221-2222

Has an outdoor pool, continental breakfast and a 2-star rating from AAA. Ask about AAA discounts.

RODEWAY INN

www.rodewayinn.com

28718 Front Street, Temecula, California 92590

(951) 676-4833

Has a pool and spa and is located about 3.5 miles from the wineries.

Bed and Breakfast Inns

A Stay at Temecula Creek Inn

A night's stay at Temecula Creek Inn (www.temeculacreekinn.com), reminded me of the high quality Enchantment resort in Sedona, Arizona that is almost twice the cost of a stay here. As with Enchantment resort, the rooms have a native American theme, although I was told they will soon renovate their rooms to have a wine country theme and will eventually put in a spa. Aveda product fans will enjoy their soaps and shampoos that are placed in the bathroom. Their Temet Grill restaurant has a view looking out to their tree-lined golf course.

A Stay at Loma Vista Bed & Breakfast

At first blush the Loma Vista Bed & Breakfast Inn appears to be like a large home, and it is in a sense. The shared guest living room features an old-fashioned-looking television (like one you'd find at Mom's). There's a large dining table where they have the most sumptuous breakfast for guests at 9 a.m. When I visited, the breakfast consisted of a starter of a smoothie-type strawberry-flavored concoction in a martini glass, followed by a ham and chicken blintz and a warm croissant. Champagne, juice, and coffee were also served, and at the end they brought out small round brownies dusted with confectioners sugar. The breakfast was the highlight for me. Not only was the food good, but the discussions with all the other guests couldn't be beat. I left with four business cards and a feeling of having been at a Thanksgiving dinner. The inn offers 10 rooms (all with different names) that overlook vineyards, and they have a Jacuzzi near the garden, which is full of roses, geraniums and various herbs and shrubs.

A stay at The Inn at Churon Winery

On a December just before Christmas, I stayed in one of the vineyard-view rooms. The room had a huge marble-covered bathroom with a large spa tub and separate shower area.

The room's fireplace could be started by the switch of a timer. The bed was a king. It had wonderfully soft cotton linens and a down-filled comforter. The furnishings were French inspired and French doors opened to a view of the vineyards. It was decorated in neutrals with touches of yellow and blues. In the morning, breakfast was served in their dining area.

A stay at a South Coast Private Villa

I experienced a stay at a South Coast private villa surrounded by grape vines. The unique concept and apartment-like room make you feel as if you're the only guest there. No other room touches your wall so that means no rowdy neighbors disturbing your sleep. The room has all the comforts for an upscale experience. A huge bathroom with tub, bathrobes and even a chilled bottle of wine in the refrigerator.

Lodging - Golf Course Resort
JUST OUTSIDE WINE COUNTRY

TEMECULA CREEK INN
www.temeculacreekin.com
44501 Rainbow Canyon Road, Temecula, California 92592
(951) 694-1000 or (800) 962-7335

Nice rooms with comfortable beds. There's a 27-hole golf course, tennis courts and a nice restaurant on the property.

Lodging - Inside Wine Country

INN AT CHURON WINERY
www.innatchuronwinery.com
33233 Rancho California Road, Temecula, California 92591
(951) 694-9070

LOMA VISTA BED & BREAKFAST
www.lomavistabb.com
33350 La Serena Way, Temecula, California 92591
(951) 676-7047

Located in the heart of the winery area overlooking grape vines.

SOUTH COAST RESORT
www.wineresort.com
34843 Rancho California Road, Temecula, California 92591
(951) 587.WINE (9463) or (866) 9.WINERY (946379)

Tours

THE GRAPELINE WINE COUNTRY SHUTTLE
www.gogrape.com
8WINERY (946379)

This is a van tour (holds about 20 passengers) through the Temecula winery area. Tours and packages available.

WEST COAST CHAUFFEUR AND TRANSPORTATION
www.wctrans.com
(951) 926-1902

This luxury transportation service offers sedans, stretch limos, SUVs and Chrysler 300s. You can purchase wine tasting packages, prepaid winery tickets and they offer specials.

SUNRIDER JEEP WINE TOURS
www.sunriderwinetours.com
(951) 551-1516

Offers a five-hour guided backcountry Jeep Tour of the Temecula Valley's wineries and vineyards.

DESTINATION TEMECULA
www.destem.com
(951) 695-1232

Offers tours of the Temecula wine country with departures from hotels in San Diego, Anaheim and Temecula.

VINO LIMOUSINES
www.vinolimo.com
(951) 551-4710

Offers chauffeur-driven wine tours from pickup locations in Temecula Valley

Temecula Wine Focused Restaurants

A number of the wineries have restaurants on their premises. Most of them use local produce when they can and match their dishes to the wines they offer. They also feature chefs that have extensive training with awards like "Chef of the Year". Most likely if you enjoy a winery's wine offerings, you'll appreciate their restaurant as well.

BLOCK FIVE RESTAURANT AT LEONESSE WINERY
www.leonessecellars.com
(951) 302-7601

Focuses on gourmet food with wines offered by the glass and bottle. Open for lunch and dinner

CAFE CHAMPAGNE AT THORNTON WINERY
www.thorntonwine.com
(951) 699-0088

Focuses on "contemporary fusion cuisine" with wine pairing suggestions. Open for lunch and dinner.

CAROL'S RESTAURANT AT BAILY VINEYARD
www.bailywinery.com
(951) 676-9463

Offers lunch dishes like salads, sandwiches and pasta and local wines by the glass. Open for lunch Wednesday through Sunday.

CREEKSIDE GRILLE AT WILSON CREEK WINERY
www.wilsoncreekwinery.com
(951) 699-9463

Creates wine country food with wine pairing in mind. Open for lunch and dinner.

MERITAGE RESTAURANT AT CALLAWAY WINERY
www.callawaywinery.com
(951) 676-4001

Focuses on wine and Mediterranean tapas food pairings. Open daily for lunch and on Friday and Saturday for dinner.

THE PINNACLE RESTAURANT AT FALKNER WINERY
www.falknerwinery.com
(951) 676-8231

Emphasizes Mediterranean style food and open daily for lunch.

TEMET GRILL AT TEMECULA CREEK INN
www.temeculacreekinn.com
(877) 517-1823

Prepares food inspired by the local vineyards. Open for breakfast, lunch and dinner.

VINEYARD ROSE RESTAURANT AT SOUTH COAST WINERY
www.wineresort.com
(866) 994-6379

Crafts seasonal dishes focused on wine-friendly selections. Open for breakfast, lunch and dinner.

Where To Buy Items For A Picnic Basket

BARON'S THE MARKETPLACE

www.baronsmarketplace.com
31939 Rancho California Road, Temecula, CA 92591
(951) 693-1111

Just before you reach the Temecula wine country you'll find Baron's The Marketplace which is stocked with everything you'll need to fill a picnic basket. There's locally produced honey, gourmet bread, bottled water, a case full of gourmet cheese, chocolate covered pretzels and other crunchy snacks. Make this stop before you wished you had.

TEMECULA VALLEY CHEESE COMPANY

42072 5th Street, #10, Temecula, CA 92591
(951) 693-9500

Located in the Old Town area of Temecula, you can order sandwiches made with meats and cheeses that are rotated depending on availability. When I was there the supply included cured meats like salami, coppa, pancetta and sopressata. They offer cheeses like gouda, goat cheddar, sage derby, and fresh chevre as well as olives like gordals and kalamatas.

Temecula Valley Chamber of Commerce
www.temecula.org
(951) 676-5090

Temecula Valley Wine Growers Association
(951) 699-6586 or (800) 801-9463.
Call to request a brochure about the wine country.

Temecula wineries offering wholesale and by appointment tastings. Please call to make an appointment to visit them.

Boorman Vineyards

www.boormanvineyards.com

Focusing on premium red varieties like Cabernet Sauvignon, Cabernet Franc and Petit Verdot. Call for an appointment (951) 600-9333.

Chapin Family Vineyards

Owned by Steve Chapin this winery currently offers Syrah and Cabernet Sauvignon. Special tours by appointment only. (760) 473-7704

Gershon Bachus Vintners

www.gershonbachus.com
(877) 458-8428

Open on some Saturdays and Sundays. They offer limited production wines.

Lumiere Winery

www.lumierewinery.com

39555 Calle Contento, Temecula, CA 92591 (951) 676-7022

Temecula Wineries

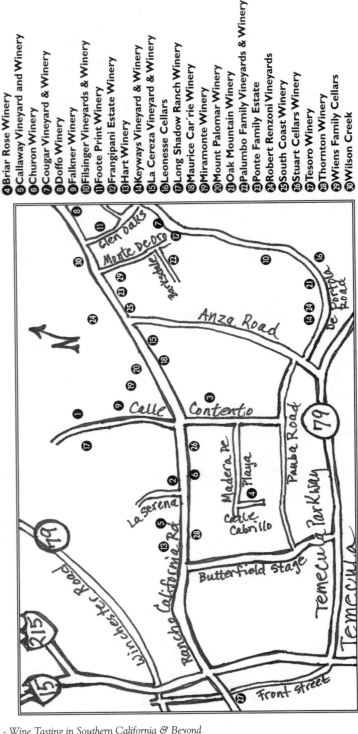

1. Alex's Red Barn Winery
2. Baily Vineyard & Winery
3. Bella Vista Winery
4. Briar Rose Winery
5. Callaway Vineyard and Winery
6. Churon Winery
7. Cougar Vineyard & Winery
8. Doffo Winery
9. Falkner Winery
10. Filsinger Vineyards & Winery
11. Foote Print Winery
12. Frangipani Estate Winery
13. Hart Winery
14. Keyways Vineyard & Winery
15. La Cereza Vineyard & Winery
16. Leonesse Cellars
17. Long Shadow Ranch Winery
18. Maurice Car'rie Winery
19. Miramonte Winery
20. Mount Palomar Winery
21. Oak Mountain Winery
22. Palumbo Family Vineyards & Winery
23. Ponte Family Estate
24. Robert Renzoni Vineyards
25. South Coast Winery
26. Stuart Cellars Winery
27. Tesoro Winery
28. Thornton Winery
29. Wiens Family Cellars
30. Wilson Creek

Alex's Red Barn Winery

Alex and Lise Yakut own this 25-acre estate vineyard where they produce Old Vine Sauvignon Blanc, Old Vine Cabernet Sauvignon (a gold medal winner), Old-Vine Johannisberg Riesling, Solera style Sherry, Viognier and Syrah. Originally a demonstration vineyard to showcase the grape growing capabilities to land buyers, the original vines included Johannisberg Riesling, Sauvignon Blanc and Cabernet Sauvignon. Most of the wines are produced from grapes grown on their vineyard

 LOCATION: 39820 Calle Contento, Temecula, California 92591 (951) 693-3201

 WEBSITE: www.redbarnwine.com

 TASTING ROOM HOURS: Weekends and most holidays: Summer 11 a.m. to 6 p.m., Winter 10 a.m. to 5 p.m.

 TOURS: No

 TASTING CHARGE: Yes

 WINE FOCUS: Old Vine and Solera style Sherry

 DIRECTIONS: Take I-15 and exit at Rancho California Road. Head east. Calle Contento is a cross street of Rancho California Road. Make a left at Calle Contento. The winery is on the right just past Falkner Winery.

Baily Vineyard & Winery

The vine covered winery's grey stone building looks as though it might be a tasting room in Europe or Napa Valley. Their gift shop features lots of gargoyles and you'll find them in Carol's Restaurant as well as on the outside of the building. A walk toward the tasting room features a demonstration garden.

The winery began in 1986 by a former computer software developer, his wife, and their two sons. The owners, Phil and Carol Baily, operate not only Baily Vineyard & Winery but also Carol's Restaurant. There's a gift shop across from the tasting room offering unique items for sale. Occasionally winemaker dinners are offered featuring special menus that enhance local wines. Carol's restaurant offers a warm and inviting atmosphere.

Their '99 Merlot garnered an 88 in *Wine Spectator*.

 LOCATION:
33440 La Serena, Temecula, California   92591
(951) 676-9463

 WEBSITE: www.bailywinery.com

 TASTING ROOM HOURS: 11 a.m. to 5 p.m. Monday through Friday and Sunday; Saturday 10 a.m. to 5 p.m.

 TOURS: No

 TASTING CHARGE: Yes

 WINE FOCUS: Bordeaux

 DIRECTIONS: To get to the tasting room, take I-15, exit at Rancho California Road, and head east. The winery will be on the left just past La Serena.

Bella Vista Winery

Bella Vista Winery was the first commercial vineyard in Temecula when it was named Cilurzo Winery. Currently owned by Imre and Gizella Cziraki, the winery has the distinction of being the only one in the valley to boast organic wines. Since the sharp shooter, that angry critter that wreaks havoc on grape vines, was such a menace in the not-too-distant past, they say that they still have to spray the vines, "only we use an organic spray."

They achieved a gold medal for their 2003 Petite Sirah from the San Francisco International competition.

 LOCATION: 41220 Calle Contento, Temecula, California 92592 (951) 676-5250

 WEBSITE: www.cilurzowine.com

 HOURS: 10 a.m. to 5 p.m. daily.

 TOURS: Yes

 TASTING CHARGE: Yes

 WINE FOCUS: Organic wine

 DIRECTIONS: Take I-15 to Rancho California Road and head east about 5 miles. Make a right on Calle Contento. The winery is located on Calle Contento.

Briar Rose Winery

Take the time to make an appointment to visit the husband and wife owned Briar Rose Winery. The Disneyland-looking gingerbread home hosts the tasting room. The owners, Les and Dorian Linkogle seem as though they were made to live here as a Snow White-looking Dorian often is the greeter. As it turns out the Disney theme is from the previous owner who worked there. The standout factor of this winery is the winemaker's creativity. Les, the winemaker, has been coming up with a unique innovative lemon accentuated Viognier sipping wine called Citronier. He's also created what he's calling a light lager wine. It's stored in kegs, like beer, and has a huge foamy head. Les says there are health benefits to it because of the grape enzymes that are part of the drink. The creativity also goes toward making premium, unique varietal style wines like Cabernet Sauvignon, Petite Verdot and Cabernet Franc. This helped them receive an invitation from the White House to attend a Library of Congress dinner where they presented a 1997 Cabernet Sauvignon.

 LOCATION: 41720 Calle Cabrillo, Temecula, California 92592

 WEBSITE: www.briarrosewinery.com

 HOURS: By appointment

 TOURS: Yes

 TASTING CHARGE: Yes

 WINE FOCUS: Ultra premium, handcrafted wine

 DIRECTIONS: Take I-15 to Rancho California Road and head east. Make a right at Butterfield Stage Road and a left at Madera de Playa. Take a right at Calle Cabrillo.

Callaway Vineyard and Winery

Callaway winery was founded by Ely Callaway in 1969, who may be most noted for his fame and fortune in the world of golf. That year he started the first winery in the Temecula Valley and situated it on a 1600-foot plateau overlooking the rolling hills of the valley.

The winery's focus on fruit-forward wine that pairs well with food has given the winery a distinction in Temecula. The Meritage restaurant offers al fresco dining with panoramic vineyard views. In the past you could find their wines at stores throughout the Southern California region, but now you'll have to stop by the winery or order the wine online. They hold special wine and food events throughout the year. Check their website for listings.

 LOCATION: 32720 Rancho California Road, Temecula, California 92591
(951) 676-4001 or 1 (800) 472-2377

 WEBSITE: www.callawaywinery.com

 TASTING ROOM HOURS: 10 a.m. to 5 p.m. daily

 TOURS: Yes, complimentary

 TASTING CHARGE: Yes

 WINE FOCUS: Approachable, flavorful balanced wines that are food friendly

 DIRECTIONS: Take I-15 to the Rancho California Road exit. Head east for about 4 miles. The winery is on the left.

The Inn at Churon Winery

This French Chateau inspired winery features a sweeping staircase leading up to the inn that makes you feel as if you're starring in *Gone with the Wind*. A night's stay here includes a full breakfast in the morning. The tasting room is spacious and offers an array of tasting choices including a Gold medal winning '05 Petite Sirah, Silver medal winning '05 Cabernet/Mouverdre, Silver medal winning '05 Malbec and an '03 Vin Rouge that won a Bronze Medal. All their medals come from the Temecula Valley Wine Society.

 LOCATION: 33233 Rancho California Road, Temecula, California 92591 (951) 694-9070

 WEBSITE www.innatchuronwinery.com

 TASTING HOURS: Daily from 10:00 a.m. to 4:30 p.m.

 TOURS: No

 TASTING CHARGE: Yes

 WINE FOCUS: Reds

 DIRECTIONS: Take I-15 to the Rancho California Road exit. Head east. The winery and inn are on the right side, after Thornton Winery.

Cougar Vineyard & Winery

Cougar Vineyard and Winery opened in November 2006 on the Deportola trail that is starting to sprout a bunch of wineries. Their warehouse-like building proves their philosophy of focusing on wine-making in small production. Their goal is to use most of their own grapes to produce all their wines in just a few years. They extend their arms to everyone who wants to visit–allowing offsite food at their picnic benches and welcoming big groups. They sponsor live music every Saturday. Their Sangiovese is a good bet.

LOCATION: 39870 De Portola Road, Temecula, California 92592 (951) 491-0825

WEBSITE www.cougarvineyards.com

TASTING HOURS: Daily 11 a.m. to 6 p.m.

TOURS: Yes

TASTING CHARGE: Yes

WINE FOCUS: Italian varieties

DIRECTIONS: Take I-15 to Rancho California Road east. Make a right at Glenoaks Road and a right at De Portola Road. The winery is the first one you'll meet on De Portola.

Doffo Winery

Doffo Winery is owned by Marcelo Doffo, a native of Italy who grew up in a small farming community in Argentina. He's proud of producing 100% Estate grown wine. Doffo is a small winery that specializes in high quality red wines. They produce less than 1000 cases a year and their focus is all about the wine. You'll find Cabernet Sauvignon, Syrah, Malbec and Zinfandel here.

 LOCATION: 36083 Summitville, Temecula, California 92592 (951) 676-6989 or (714) 715-6610

 WEBSITE www.doffowines.com

 TASTING HOURS: 10 a.m. to 5 p.m. Friday through Sunday and Holidays

 TOURS: No

 TASTING CHARGE: Yes

 WINE FOCUS: Small lot, handcrafted wines

 DIRECTIONS: Take I-15 to the Rancho California Road exit. Head east. Doffo's is at the far end of Rancho after Wilson Creek Winery.

Falkner Winery

Falkner Winery sits at the top of a hill like a King's castle overlooking its constituency. The owners Ray and Loretta Falkner are a vital force of the winery–hands-on making the wine and planning weddings and events. They have a restaurant on the premises, called Pinnacle Restaurant, they offer wine classes like "Introduction to Wine" and "Advanced Tasting" and on Sunday afternoons they have free jazz.

The *Wine Enthusiast* rated their '99 Amante a 93 and their 2000 Sauvignon Blanc an 86 out of 100.

 LOCATION: 40620 Calle Contento, Temecula, California 92591 (951) 676-8231

 WEBSITE: www.falknerwinery.com

 HOURS: Daily 10 a.m. to 5 p.m.

 TOURS: Yes

 TASTING CHARGE: Yes

 WINE FOCUS: Fruit forward whites and rich, smooth reds

 DIRECTIONS: Take I-15 and exit at Rancho California Road. Head east. Calle Contento is a cross street of Rancho California Road. Make a left at Calle Contento. The winery is on the right.

Filsinger Vineyards & Winery

For a winery that wants to hide out from the crowd, it stands out anyway for its quality wines and a down-to-earth approach to wine tasting. Filsinger Vineyards & Winery began in 1980 by Dr. Bill Filsinger, Kathy Filsinger and Eric Filsinger (the assistant winemaker).

The winery doesn't search out wine tasters, but wine tasters should search them out. The Filsinger family has roots in Germany, and had a winery there before World War II. They decided to start a winery in Temecula in the German tradition, and they claim to be one of the first wineries in Southern California to grow and produce Gerwürtztraminer.

 LOCATION: 39050 De Portola Road, Temecula, California 92592 (951) 302-6363

 WEBSITE www.filsingerwinery.com

 HOURS: 10 a.m. to 5 p.m. weekends and 11 a.m. to 4 p.m. Fridays

 TOURS: Yes

 TASTING CHARGE: Yes

 WINE FOCUS: Old California style wine with full varietal character

 DIRECTIONS: Head east on Rancho California Road and make a right on Glenoaks Road (Glenoaks Road is about 10 miles from I-15). Make a right on De Portola Road.

Foote Print Winery
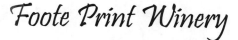

Foote Print Winery is family owned and operated and stresses that they are "bare bones, no frills. It's like coming to a farm." The winery is in a steel barn. They are a certified organic farm producing fruit that's available throughout the year. Some of their wines have won awards including a Bronze for their '05 Port from the Orange County Fair.

 LOCATION: 36650 Glenoaks Road, Temecula, California 92592 (951) 265-9951

 WEBSITE: www.footeprintwinery.com

 TASTING ROOM HOURS: 12 noon to 5 p.m. Friday and 10 a.m. to 5 p.m. Saturday and Sunday

 TOURS: No

 TASTING CHARGE: Yes

 WINE FOCUS: Red wine

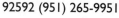 **DIRECTIONS:** Head east on Rancho California Road and make a right on Glenoaks Road (Glenoaks Road is about 10 miles from I-15).

Frangipani Estate Winery

Another new husband and wife owned, winery that has shown up on De Portola Road is Frangipani Estate Winery. Don, the winemaker and owner and his wife, JoAnn, offer a Spanish style look at their winery. They produce about 4,000 cases of wine per year and focus on red wines like Cabernet Sauvignon, Petite Syrah and Cabernet Franc. Possibly too new to have produced award winning wines just yet, their Petite Syrah shows promise.

 LOCATION: 39750 De Portola Road, Temecula, California 92592 (951) 699-8845

 WEBSITE: www.frangipaniwinery.com

 HOURS: 10 a.m. to 5 p.m. daily

 TOURS: No

 TASTING CHARGE: Yes

 WINE FOCUS: Red wine

DIRECTIONS: Head east on Rancho California Road and make a right on Glenoaks Road (Glenoaks Road is about 10 miles from I-15). Make a right on De Portola Road. Frangipani is located after Cougar Winery.

Hart Winery

Sitting down with Joe Hart of Hart Winery proves that some wineries don't need a grand entrance, large gift shop or spa to attract visitors. Back in 1973, before most others placed roots a year later, Hart was planning his vineyard. With his long-vision, he's proven that a winery can be successful, by guess what: making high quality wine. Their silver medal winning Grenache Rosé is still one of their mainstays. Hart Winery looks like a place you might find in the Old West but it was started in 1980. The tasting room is located in a small building with a porch that looks as though it's waiting for some horses to be tied to it. The Wall Street Journal named Hart Winery's rosé wine one of its favorite brands. The newspaper found only three rosés in America that were "excellent" and one of those bottles came from Hart Winery. It turns out Hart's Grenache Rosé wine wins awards every year at the Los Angeles County Fair. You'll probably have to visit the winery in order to purchase a bottle because the wines are produced on a limited basis.

LOCATION: 41300 Avenida Biona, Temecula, California 92591 (951) 676-6300

WEBSITE: www.thehartfamilywinery.com

TASTING HOURS: 9 a.m. to 4:30 p.m. daily

TOURS: Yes

TASTING CHARGE: Yes

WINE FOCUS: Small lot, quality wine

DIRECTIONS: From I-15, exit Rancho California Road. Go east. It's the first winery on the left. Avenida Biona is actually the winery's driveway.

Keyways Vineyard & Winery

Keyways Vineyard & Winery greets guests with a broad lawn-lined entrance and views of hillsides and grape vines. The tasting room feels as though you've stepped into an upscale ski lodge. It's clear with the attention-to-detail this winery offers that a female owns this one. Terri Pebley, the owner, says she's the only woman-owned and managed winery in Southern California. She said Carl Keys, the previous owner, talked her into buying the property. She replanted the vineyard and now produces enough grapes to make her own estate wines. Another feminine touch this winery offers is a focus on award winning sweet wines. Their late harvest Sauvignon Blanc Sweet Surrender is a good alternative to dessert. They produce 10,000 cases a year.

LOCATION: 37338 De Portola Road, Temecula, California 92592 (951) 302-7888

WEBSITE: www.keywayswine.com

HOURS: 10 a.m. to 6 p.m. daily.

TOURS: Yes, with advanced reservations

TASTING CHARGE: Yes

WINE FOCUS: Rhone varietals

DIRECTIONS: Take I-15 to Rancho California Road east. Turn South on Anza road and travel 2.6 miles. Turn left on De Portola Road. Located about 2.1 miles on the left.

La Cereza Vineyard & Winery

Founded in 1994, La Cereza Vineyard & Winery is currently owned by Buddy and Cheri Linn. The Spanish style setting includes picnic grounds overlooking vineyards. The winemaker focuses on small quantity, boutique wines and creates a multitude of varietal and blended wines. They offer gourmet cheeses and deli items along with 22 varietal wines like Chardonnay, Zinfandel and a wine called Girlfriends that's meant to appeal to a female palate. Their Grenache has won Gold and Silver medals and their Gewurztraminer has won multiple Gold medals.

 LOCATION: 34567 Rancho California Road, Temecula, California 92592 (951) 699-6961

 WEBSITE: www.lacerezawinery.com

 HOURS: 10 a.m. to 5 p.m. daily

 TOURS: No

 TASTING CHARGE: Yes

 WINE FOCUS: Small quantity, boutique wines

 DIRECTIONS: Take I-15 to the Rancho California Road exit. Head east on Rancho California Road. The winery is located on the right, approximately 7 miles from the freeway.

Leonesse Cellars

The views from the elegantly designed tasting room look out onto mountains that are sometimes capped in snow during the winter time. The tasting room is comforting with a fireplace and seating areas. The winery offers a range of varietal wines with the Wine Enthusiast giving 90 points for their '05 vineyard release Syrah and their '04 Merlot receiving 90 points from the Wine Connoisseur. Wine club members can enjoy a Barrel Room experience where they may relax on sofas and chairs surrounded by rustic tables and wine barrels.

 LOCATION: 38311 De Portola Road, Temecula, California 92592 (951) 302-7601

 WEBSITE: www.leonessecellars.com

 HOURS: Daily 11 a.m. to 5 p.m.

 TOURS: Yes, with reservation

 TASTING CHARGE: Yes

 WINE FOCUS: Rhone style

 DIRECTIONS: Take I-15 to Rancho California Road east. Turn South on Anza road. Turn left on De Portola Road.

Long Shadow Ranch Winery

Surrounded by horses and white ranch-style fencing, Long Shadow Ranch Winery sits next to Falkner Winery. Here you'll find a park-like setting with picnic tables near horse stables; a white carriage sits on the grass-covered area. The tasting room is small and intimate, and reminds me of a tasting room you might find tucked into a corner of Sonoma Valley.

Perhaps this winery's distinction is in its offering of horse-drawn carriage wine tasting trips. Their Belgian draft horses will take you through vineyards around Temecula.

 WINERY TASTING ROOM: 39847 Calle Contento, Temecula, California 92591 (951) 587-6221
OLD TOWN TASTING ROOM: 28500 Old Town Street, Temecula, California 92590 (951) 699-1600

 WEBSITE: www.Longshadowranchwinery.com

 WINERY TASTING HOURS: Monday through Friday 12 noon to 5 p.m., Saturday and Sunday 10 a.m. to 5 p.m.
OLD TOWN TASTING HOURS: Monday through Thursday, 12 noon to 7 p.m., Friday 11 a.m. to 10 p.m., Saturday 10 a.m. to 11 p.m. Sunday 12 noon to 7 p.m.

 TOURS: No

 TASTING CHARGE: Yes

 WINE FOCUS: Reds

 DIRECTIONS: Take I-15 toward Temecula, exit at Rancho California Road heading east. Make a left at Calle Contento.

Maurice Carrie Winery

Maurice Cafrie is like the Southern Belle of the Temecula wineries. Maybe it's the gazebo, lawn and rose bushes out front–or perhaps it's the friendly people. Or it could be the bustling atmosphere inside. Started in 1986 by Maurice and Bud Van Roekel, the winery is comfortable and homey. The Van Roekel's established the first vineyard in the region planting grapes in 1968. By 1986, they built the Victorian-era style winery, and currently sell about 25,000 cases of wine annually.

There's lots of merchandise for sale in addition to the wine such as sourdough bread baked on the premises (one type has brie baked inside). There's also a picnic area.

 LOCATION: 34225 Rancho California Road, Temecula, California 92591 (951) 676-1711

 WEBSITE: www.mauricecarriewinery.com

 HOURS: 10 a.m. to 5 p.m. daily

TOURS: Yes

 TASTING CHARGE: Yes

WINE FOCUS: Wines that are ready to drink at an early age

 DIRECTIONS: Take I-15 and exit at Rancho California Road. Head east on Rancho California Road. The winery is about 6 miles from the freeway on the right side.

Miramonte Winery

Miramonte is located on an elevation of 1,400 feet surrounded by 12 acres of vineyards. The winery produces 5,000 cases of wine a year and focuses on Rhône varieties. They make wine with minimal intervention to bring out the natural characters of the grapes.

The owner, Cane Vanderhoof, found the winery in 2001 and was just 32 at the time.

Their 2004 Estate Syrah won a Gold at the Los Angeles County Fair and a Silver at the Pacific Rim Wine Competition.

 LOCATION: 33410 Rancho California Road, Temecula, California 92591 (951) 506-5500

 WEBSITE: www.miramontewinery.com

 HOURS: 10 a.m. to 4:45 p.m. daily

 TOURS: No

 TASTING CHARGE: Yes

 WINE FOCUS: Rhone varieties

 DIRECTIONS: Take I-15 to the Rancho California Road exit. Miramonte Winery is on the left side of the road as you head east and is located past the Loma Vista Bed & Breakfast.

Mount Palomar Winery

As one of the pioneers of the Temecula Valley, Mount Palomar has been growing and producing wines since 1969. Situated on 315 acres there are 50 acres of vineyards, fountains and flowers, a winemaking facility and four indoor and outdoor tasting bars. They've been one of the Temecula Valley's leaders in testing new grape varieties like the white Cortese which is originally from Northwest Italy.

Some recent awards include a Gold in the '08 Indy International for their Mount Palomar '05 Merlot and their '04 vintage Syrah won a best of class at the '08 California State Fair. Their '06 Riesling won a Gold at the '08 Los Angeles County Fair and Indy International. There's a deli that sells everything from sandwiches and pizza to salads.

 LOCATION: 33820 Rancho California Road, Temecula, California 92591 (951) 676-5047

 WEBSITE: www.mountpalomar.com

 HOURS: Summer: Monday through Thursday, 10 a.m. to 6 p.m. and Friday through Sunday 10 a.m. to 7 p.m. Winter: Monday through Thursday, 10 a.m. to 5 p.m., Friday and Saturday, 10 a.m. to 6 p.m. and Sunday 11 a.m. to 6 p.m.

 TOURS: Yes, guided tours at set times

 TASTING CHARGE: Yes

 WINE FOCUS: Solera Crème Sherry hand-made in one of the last outdoor soleras in California; Limited Reserve Port; Castelleto Cortese and Castelleto Sangiovese

 DIRECTIONS: From I-15 exit at Rancho California Road and drive east. The winery is about 5 miles down the road and on the left.

Port & Sherry ☆

some food weekends

Oak Mountain Winery

Located on the De Portola wine trail, Oak Mountain sits high on a hill looking toward views of Oak Mountain. The winery also produces wine for Temecula Hills Winery which now has a tasting room in Old Town. Both wineries are owned by Stephen and Valerie Andrews. Valerie describes their idea to start the wineries as "a hobby out-of-control". They have been growing unique varieties like Petit Verdot, Cabernet Franc, Malbec and Counoise. Their '05 Port garnered a Best of Show and Best of Class at the Jerry Mead International Competition and their '03 Port received a Gold Chairmans Award Unanimous at the '06 Riverside Wine Competition. They strive to produce 6,500 cases a year.

 WINERY LOCATION: 36522 Via Verde, Temecula, California 92592 (951) 699-9102
TEMECULA HILLS TASTING ROOM: 41955 Main Street, California 92590 (951) 695-4525

 WEBSITE: www.oakmountainwinery.com

 HOURS: Daily 11 a.m. to 5 p.m.

 TOURS: No

 TASTING CHARGE: Yes

 WINE FOCUS: Classic Bordeaux

 DIRECTIONS: Take I-15 to the Rancho California Road east exit. At Anza Road turn right and drive about three miles to De Portola Road. Make a left at De Portola. Make a left at Via Verde.

Muscat
Chardonnay
GSM

Palumbo Family Vineyards & Winery

The Palumbo Family Vineyards would be easy to miss if it weren't for the wine barrel out front with a sign saying "winery" pointing to the driveway. This is a small winery producing 2,500 cases per year. Grapes are grown on 13 acres surrounding the tasting room and family's home. Nicholas Palumbo along with his wife Cindy and four children are all part of the winery with Nicholas acting as the Viticulturist. He understands the value of quality wine and has decided to focus on red (mostly French variety) wines. They are dedicated to growing small-lot, handcrafted wines. If you like intimate gatherings, they offer small wine lunches that include tastings and discussions about their wines.

 LOCATION: 40150 Barksdale Circle, Temecula, California 92591 (951) 676-7900

 WEBSITE: www.palumbofamilyvineyards.com

 HOURS: Friday, 12 noon to 5 p.m., Saturday, 10 a.m to 5 p.m.

 TOURS: No

 TASTING CHARGE: Yes

 WINE FOCUS: Red wines

 DIRECTIONS: Take Rancho California Road east to Monte de Oro Road. Make a right. Make another right at Barksdale Circle. Look for the wine barrel directing you.

Ponte Family Estate

Don't like wine. Food marginal.

This winery might encourage a new interior design idea called "farmhouse chic" with a barn look and scent inside the tasting room that's so appealing I kept picking up and smelling items in the shop to determine where it was coming from! A high open ceiling in the large tasting area greets visitors at the door and the shop is full of rooster and wine memorabilia. The winery's restaurant "Smokehouse Cafe" offers dishes like lobster risotto, lemon stuffed trout and duck confit pizza with ingredients secured from local farms.

The tasting room is surrounded by 350 acres of vineyards. Look for special events such as cooking classes and wine and cigar receptions.

A unique feature of this winery is the restored chapel cellar and barrel room. Its stone front is reminiscent of buildings seen in Europe, and the stones look as though they could've come from the ground nearby.

 LOCATION: 35053 Rancho California Road, Temecula California 92591 (951) 694-8855

WEBSITE: www.pontewinery.com

HOURS: Daily 10 a.m. to 5 p.m.

TOURS: Yes

 TASTING CHARGE: Yes

 WINE FOCUS: Italian and Bordeaux wine

 DIRECTIONS: Take I-15 to the Rancho California Road exit. The winery is located on the right, heading east, after South Coast Winery.

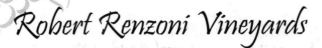

Robert Renzoni Vineyards

Robert Renzoni, the proprietor, says he has spent his entire career working in the wine industry. He comes from a long line, four generations, of wine professionals. The tasting room is currently located in a warehouse-like building on the De Portola trail. There are plans to build a Tuscan Villa tasting room. Wine is produced in limited quantities currently. They've received a Silver medal for their '07 Pinot Grigio from the Riverside Wine Competition.

 LOCATION: 37350 De Portola Road, Temecula, California 92592 (951) 302-8466

 WEBSITE: www.robertrenzonivineyards.com

 TASTING ROOM HOURS: 11 a.m to 6 p.m. daily

 TOURS: Yes, by appointment

 TASTING CHARGE: Yes

 WINE FOCUS: Italian wine

 DIRECTIONS: Take I-15 to Temecula. Head East on Rancho California Road. Turn South on Anza. Turn left at De Portola Road just past Keyways Winery.

South Coast Winery Resort & Spa

South Coast Winery is a full service destination with a tasting room, a restaurant called Vineyard Rose featuring California cuisine, a spa called GrapeSeed with scrumptious sounding treatments like Champagne facials and bungalow rooms with Jacuzzi tubs, plush robes and fireplaces to spend the night. The corner lot location has a panoramic view of the mountains surrounding the area and a rustic wood trellis lines the path to the tasting room from the parking area. The winery uses 95% estate grown grapes from their own vineyards located in both Temecula and in the valley near Palomar Mountain for their wines. Some of their recent Gold medal winners from the 2009 San Francisco Chronicle Wine Competition include Best of Class Sweepstakes Gold for their '07 Grenache Rose, a Gold for their Black Jack Port and a Gold for their Gewurtraminer.

LOCATION: 34843 Rancho California Road, Temecula California 92591 (951) 587-9463 *Good food.*

WEBSITE: www.WineResort.com

TASTING ROOM HOURS: 10 a.m to 6 p.m. weekends.

TOURS: Yes

TASTING CHARGE: Yes

WINE FOCUS: Soft, sultry, full bodied wine *very good. Bought.*

DIRECTIONS: Take I-15 to Temecula. Take the Rancho California Road exit. Head east. Located on the right hand side at the corners of Rancho California Road and Anza Road.

Stuart Cellars Winery

Stuart Cellars opened in 1998 with their first harvest from their 40 acre vineyard in 1999. You'll find a treasure inside the tasting room where an Old World experience allows you to walk on gorgeous tile while rich tapestries line the walls of the room. The tasting room is painted with warm, friendly colors. Their vineyard is planted in the French tradition which allows grapes to age evenly on each side of the vine and offers more fruit consistency. It also helps to protect the grapes from the hot summer sun by providing a canopy.

Another family owned and operated winery in the valley, it was founded by Marshall and Susan Stuart and their three children. Their '06 Syrah won a Double Gold, Best of Class at the San Francisco Chronicle 2008 wine Competition. Other varieties you'll find here are Chardonnay, Viognier, White Merlot, Cabernet Franc, Malbec and Sangiovese.

 LOCATION: 33515 Rancho California Road, Temecula, California 92591 (951) 676-6414

 WEBSITE: www.stuartcellars.com

 HOURS: 10 a.m. to 5 p.m. daily

 TOURS: Yes

 TASTING CHARGE: Yes

 WINE FOCUS: Quality wine in the Old world blended with California style

DIRECTIONS: Take I-15 to the Rancho California Road exit. Head east. Stuart Cellars Winery is located just past Thornton Winery on the right side of the road.

Tesoro Winery

The tasting room in Old Town offers live music most weekends. The owners, Kim and Buzz Olson bought land on Rancho California Road and are developing the 20 acres into an Italian winery and bed & breakfast.

 TASTING ROOM LOCATION: 28475 Old Town Front Street, Temecula, California 92590 (951) 308-0000

 WEBSITE: www.tesorowines.com

 HOURS: Monday through Thursday 12 noon to 7 p.m., Friday and Saturday 10 a.m. to 10 p.m.

 TOURS: No

 TASTING CHARGE: Yes

 WINE FOCUS: Premium Mediterranean style wines

 DIRECTIONS: Take I-15 and exit at Rancho California Road. Head West on Rancho California Road and make a left at Old Town Front Street.

Thornton Winery

Thornton Winery opened in 1988 and is a classic in the area with its longstanding focus on quality sparkling and fine wine. The winery's European look continues to the manicured herb garden that the chefs at the winery's restaurant, Cafe Champagne, use to prepare meals.

Thornton hosts events like the Champagne Jazz series on Sundays.

You'll find award winning Syrahs, Viogniers, Zinfandels and Sangiovese wines here along with the sparkling wines they're known for. Thornton's wines are easily found at area wine shops and stores, but it's hard not to stop by this impressive winery. Learn about their "méthode champenoise" process while you're there. They use it for their sparkling wine production.

 LOCATION: 32575 Rancho California Road, Temecula, California 92591 (951) 699-0099

 WEBSITE: www.thorntonwine.com

 HOURS: 10 a.m. to 5 p.m. daily

 TOURS: Yes, on the weekend

 TASTING CHARGE: Yes

WINE FOCUS: Premium wines and champagnes

 DIRECTIONS: Take I-15 and exit at Rancho California Road. The winery is located 4 miles east. It's the first winery on the right.

Wiens Family Cellars

Wiens Family Cellars greets the visitor with an open, airy, tasting room and an adjacent inviting-looking barrel room next to it that's reserved for wine club members. The winery is a family affair with Doug Wiens acting as winemaker and viticulturist while his three brothers have been involved in the designing and engineering of the facilities and handle the finances.

They produce big red wines like Barbera, Cabernet Sauvignon, Syrah and Zinfandel. They also produce whites like Chardonnay, Viognier and Pinot Gris. Most of their wines are made with grapes grown on their 70 acres of local vineyards.

 LOCATION: 35055 Via Del Ponte, Temecula, California 92592 (951) 694-9892

 WEBSITE: www.wienscellars.com

 HOURS: 10 a.m. to 5 p.m. daily

 TOURS: Yes, by appointment on Saturdays and Sundays at 11 a.m.

 TASTING CHARGE: Yes

 WINE FOCUS: Big Red Temecula wines

 DIRECTIONS: Take I-15 to the Rancho California Road exit. Head east on Rancho California Road. The winery is located about 7 miles from the freeway.

Wilson Creek Winery & Vineyards

Wilson Creek Winery is known around town as the winery that has the almond champagne—or more technically, sparkling wine. But there's more to this family endeavor than just that. There's also a conference center and restaurant, Creekside Grille, on the premises of this popular destination. Like most of the wineries in the valley, Wilson is family-owned with eight members working at the winery and a number of family members living on-site. They bought the 20-acre property in 1996 and built the winery in 1998. Currently, they produce about 30,000 cases of wine per year. Some of their recent award winning wines that have garnered Gold medals are the '08 Grenache Rosé and the '07 Petite Sirah from the Diego International Wine Competition A white gazebo on the front lawn is surrounded by roses and flowers, and a creek where you can occasionally spot ducks and frogs.

 LOCATION: 35960 Rancho California Road, Temecula, California 92591 (951) 699-9463

 WEBSITE: www.wilsoncreekwinery.com

 HOURS: 10 a.m. to 5 p.m. daily

 TOURS: Yes

 TASTING CHARGE: Yes

 WINE FOCUS: Almond Champagne

 DIRECTIONS: Take I-15 to the Rancho California Road exit. Head east on Rancho California Road. The winery is located on the left, one of the furthest wineries to the east.

Laguna Beach

There are two wineries in Laguna Beach, a beautiful coastal city in Orange County. One thing Laguna Beach is known for is the Pageant of the Masters, an art event. The buildings that line Laguna Canyon Road stand like monuments to the Pageant as it waits for the next performance. The Highway 133 drive toward the beach feels like a vacation as you move away from the industrial side of Orange County to the sage brush covered rolling hills of the burgeoning coast line. Art galleries, antique stores and garlic-emitting restaurants line the path toward the coast. When I was there, the coastline stores were covered in white lights. It felt like a fairy tale coastline.

If you're driving up the coast from the South on Pacific Coast Highway the name changes to South Coast Highway as you drive into Laguna Beach. You'll find lots of hiking trails at the **Laguna Coast Wilderness Park** (www.ocparks.com/lagunacoast). If you want to stock up on wine and food books, try the **Laguna Beach Books** (www.lagunabeachbooks.com) store at 1200 South Coast Highway, Laguna Beach (949) 494-4779

Wine Focused Restaurants
(Wine Spectator Awarded)

LAGUNA SAPPHIRE RESTAURANT
Award of Excellence
www.sapphirellc.com
1200 South Coast Highway Suite 105B, Laguna Beach, CA 92651
(949) 715-9888

Offers a relaxed, artistic setting in the original site of a landmark Pottery Shack that incorporates the feel of Laguna Beach. If you like sampling a bit of everything, their lunch box special gives you a taste of five menu samples. Happy hour offers tapas style menu items. Sapphire's wine list was recognized by *Wine Spectator* as a winner for an award of excellence. They offer a balance of old and new world producers with a wide selection of regions and varietals by the glass.

HUSH
www.hushrestaurant.com
858 South Coast Highway, Laguna Beach, CA 92651
(949) 497-3616

Offers contemporary American cuisine, a best of award of excellence from *Wine Spectator* magazine for their extensive wine list and an elegant, inviting atmosphere.

Unique Restaurant
STUDIO AT MONTAGE
www.studiolagunabeach.com
30801 South Coat Highway, Laguna Beach, CA 92651
(949) 715-6420

Studio is a restaurant that sits on the Montage Resort property overlooking the beach. They've been noted by James Beard for the best chef. They offer more than 2,200 wine labels and have a seasonal, changing menu.

Where To Buy Items For A Picnic Basket

Next door to Sapphire Restaurant you'll find,
SAPPHIRE PANTRY (949) 715-9889 with everything you'll need to pack for a picnic while touring the wineries. The shop received a "Best Cheese Shop" award from an '08 Orange Coast Magazine. Here you'll find coffee, chocolates, smoked meats, an array of deli salads and cheeses, like vintage gouda, gruyere and blue stilton.

WHOLE FOODS

www.wholefoodmarkets.com
283 Broadway Street, Laguna Beach, CA 92651
(949) 376-7888

Laguna Wine Bars

ENO WINE BAR

www.enowinerooms.com
One Ritz-Carlton Drive, Dana Point, CA 92629
(949) 240-2000

Located inside the Ritz Carlton, Eno is an upscale wine tasting room. Offers Eno-versity classes focusing on both novice and expert wine connoisseurs.

Retail Store

Not far from the beach and just a mile or two from the Laguna Canyon winery is the California Taste Fine Wine store.

CALIFORNIA TASTE FINE WINE

www.caltaste.com
303 Broadway Suite 103, Laguna Beach, CA 92651
(949) 715-5385

They host Friday and Saturday evening wine tastings and focus on red wine drinkers.

Orange County Wine shop

WINE EXCHANGE

www.winex.com
1500 E. Village Way Suite 2364, Orange CA 92865
(714) 974-1454

On first glance, Wine Exchange looks like an expanded version of Beverages and More, but their primary focus of discounts on wine and with two times the selection of most wine stores this is a place to go to stock up your wine cellar or cabinet, at home. For example, one of their wines of the month was a Tilia 2007 Cabernet for $7.99. You won't find tourist, cutesy shops in this part of town, but you might want to clean out your trunk so you can take home the goods.

Laguna Lodging

OK, so maybe you're not Paris Hilton but you might be able to pull off acting like her for a day or two with a stay at one of these resorts.

Both are located on the coastline off of Pacific Coast Highway. With high room entry rates, your budget might allow for just a night but what the heck, it's your big birthday, anniversary, insert celebratory event here_____

Pampering

MONTAGE RESORT & SPA
www.montagelagunabeach.com
30801 South Coast Highway, Laguna Beach, CA 92651
(866) 271-6953

Montage Laguna Beach is located on 30 spectacular acres in the heart of Laguna Beach, approximately 60 minutes from both Los Angeles and San Diego and 18 miles from Orange County's John Wayne International Airport.

The resort sits on the ocean with rooms, restaurants and even workout centers that face the water. So it's hanging out at the beach minus the sand in your bathing suit and sticking to your oiled body. This hotel is not for the budget conscious but if you're looking to celebrate an occasion and splurge a bit you can do that here. Or, if you just want the experience for the day you can book a spa appointment or eat at one of the restaurants.

RITZ-CARLTON, LAGUNA NIGUEL
www.ritzcarlton.com
One Ritz-Carlton Drive, Dana Point, CA 92629
(949) 240-2000

A modern interior with clubby music greets visitors upon entrance. There's a lovely panoramic view of the ocean. Eno wine bar is here.

Laguna Beach Wineries

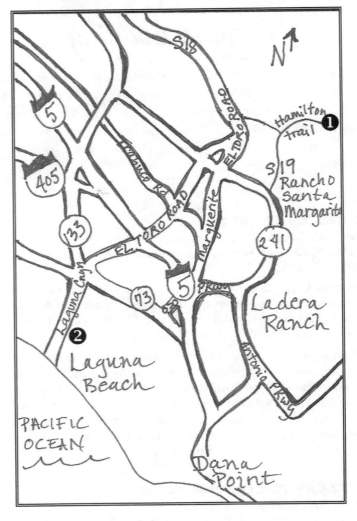

1 Hamilton Oaks Vineyards
2 Laguna Canyon Winery

Hamilton Oaks Vineyards

Scheduling an appointment-only visit with Hamilton Oaks Vineyards is worth the time. A small production (3,000 cases a year) wine output insures you'll get the time and attention of the winemaker, owner and all-around nice guy, Ron. Their '02 Cabernet Sauvignon was recognized by *Wine Spectator* but the demand from the article left the wine no longer available. Ron says that each year the wine changes as climate and other aspects affect the wine. You'll find hand crafted unique wines here. Isn't that what the search is about? Some of the local hotels coordinate tastings and van shuttles here.

 LOCATION: 31111 Hamilton Trail, Trabuco Canyon, California 92679 (949) 459-6914

 WEBSITE: www.hamiltonoaksvineyard.com

 TASTING ROOM HOURS: By appointment only, daily from 11 a.m. to 4:30 p.m. and Sunday from 12:30 p.m. to 4:30 p.m.

 TOURS: No

 WINE FOCUS: Unique, handcrafted wine

 TASTING CHARGE: Yes

 DIRECTIONS: Take I-5 toward Orange County. Exit at Oso Parkway and head East. Make a left at Marguerite Parkway and a right at El Toro Road. Then make a right at Live Oak Canyon Road and a left at Hamilton Trail.

Laguna Canyon Winery

The tasting room hosts wine barrels and a backdrop of wine bottles. Although the winery doesn't grow their own grapes (they get the grapes from Napa and Sonoma), their winemaker Darren Huber has created Bronze medal winning (Orange County Fair) Sangiovese and Pinot Noirs. I'm a Syrah fan and theirs is worthy! Darren says its one of his favorites.

 LOCATION: 2133 Laguna Canyon Road, Laguna Beach, California 92651 (949) 715-9463

 WEBSITE: www.Lagunacanyonwinery.com

 TASTING ROOM HOURS: Daily from 11 a.m. to 6 p.m., no reservation required, closed on Monday and holidays

 TOURS: No

 WINE FOCUS: Boutique wines from premium grapes

 TASTING CHARGE: Yes

 DIRECTIONS: Take the 405 or I-5 headed toward Laguna Beach and exit at 133 South. After about four or five miles the winery will be located on the left hand side of Laguna Canyon Road.

Los Angeles County

Wineries in Los Angeles County are grouped in areas. You'll find a patch in Malibu, another patch in Antelope Valley, some more in Oxnard and Ventura, then one in the heart of the city and a few in the surrounding areas of the Inland Empire.

It was just about nine years ago that a Prohibition-era ban was lifted in the Los Angeles area. Winemaking started in Los Angeles in the 1700s by Spanish missionaries who planted grapes for their missions and was the center of California winemaking in the 19th century.

Currently, L.A. winemakers are allowed to operate boutique wineries and it seems more growers pop up every day.

On your way to the Rancho Cucamonga wineries you might want to stop at **San Antonio's** additional tasting room, located at 2802 S. Miliken Avenue in Ontario (909) 947-3995. The tasting room is close to Galleano Winery.

Near the Agua Dulce Winery, you might want to check out the **Valencia Wine Company,** located at 24300 Town Center Drive #105 (661) 254-9300 or look at their website at www.valenciawine.com. The shop has a wine bar, classes, a "Meet the Winemaker" night and of course, a shop full of wine.

Los Angeles wineries
offering wholesale and by appointment tastings.
Please call to make an appointment to visit them.

Donatoni Winery

S La Cienega Blvd., Inglewood, CA 90304
(310) 645-544510604

Moraga Vineyards

www.moragavineyards.com
Located in the hills of Bel Air.
(310) 476-3051

Los Angeles County Wine Bars

Most of the wine bars in Los Angeles are located in central LA about 15 to 25 minutes from the San Antonio Winery or near the beaches and the Malibu wineries. So your best bet is to plan a trip to an area winery and then check out some of the wine bars near there. No, this is not a complete listing of every wine bar in LA, just a sampling near other wine attractions. Also, a lot of the wine focused restaurants in LA are near these areas too. A side note, as in other locales, sometimes it's hard to make a distinction between a wine bar and a restaurant as a lot of them offer both wine and food. However, wine bars, in general, make wine the main focus over food.

A.O.C

www.aocwinebar.com
8022 West Third Street, Los Angeles, CA 90048
(323) 653-6359

Offers a large selection of wines by the glass and small plate foods. A favorite of locals and out-of-towners.

BACARO L.A.

www.bacaroLA.com
2308 South Union Avenue, Los Angeles, CA 90007
(213) 748-7205

Offers cold and hot cichetti (like artisan cured meats and roasted rainbow beets) along with their wines.

BODEGA WINE BAR

www.bodegawinebar.com
260 East Colorado Boulevard, Pasadena, CA 91101
(626) 793-4300

814 Broadway (@Lincoln), Santa Monica, CA 90401
(310) 394-3504

Locations are somewhat close to either San Antonio Winery or the Malibu wineries. They feature live music in a casual, as they describe "living room-ish" atmosphere and focus on food like pizzas and finger foods along with wine that's affordable.

COLORADO WINE COMPANY

www.cowineco.com
2114 Colorado Boulevard, Los Angeles, CA 90041
(323) 478-1985

In the Eagle Rock community, not far from San Antonio Winery, this wine bar offers wines and beers from around the world and focus on bottles under $25.

CORK BAR

www.corkbar.com
403 West 12th Street, Los Angeles, CA 90015
(213) 746-0050

A new wine bar, just about four miles from San Antonio Winery, that focuses on the California wine experience and offers a large selection of wines by the glass. They also offer local beer from San Diego producers and of course food made from fresh Farmer's Market ingredients.

ENOTECA DRAGO

www.enotecadrago.blogspot.com
410 North Canon Drive, Beverly Hills, CA 90210
(310) 786-8236

A wine bar focused on Italian wine regions and made to replicate traditional wine shops. Italian wine and food available. Received an award of excellence from *Wine Spectator*.

55 DEGREE WINE

www.55degreewine.com
3111 Glendale Boulevard Suite 2, Los Angeles, CA 90039
(323) 662-5556

Has a tasting bar plus "off the beaten path" wine selections from all over the world.

MONSIEUR MARCEL RESTAURANT & WINE BAR

www.mrmarcel.com
6333 West Third Street, Los Angeles, CA 90036
(323) 939-7792

A wine bar and restaurant focused on French wine and food.

THE LITTLE DOOR

www.thelittledoor.com
8164 West Third Street, Los Angeles, CA 90048
(323) 951-1210

A romantic setting that is a restaurant and wine bar. Next door, there's not just a wine shop, but an organic bakery with pastries and more.

LOU

www.louonvine.com
724 Vine Street, Los Angeles, CA 90038
(323) 962-6369

Focused on natural winegrowing and supporting winemakers that grow grapes native to their environment, the wine list changes often as does their seasonal offering of fresh food based from local farmers markets. You'll find them in a strip mall, also native to its environment!

RUSTIC CANYON WINE BAR AND SEASONAL KITCHEN

www.rusticcanyonwinebar.com
1119 Wilshire Boulevard, Santa Monica, CA 90401
(310) 393-7050

Rustic Canyon received an Award of Excellence from *Wine Spectator*. They offer a wide range of varietal wine from the world's selections.

Los Angeles County Wine Focused Restaurants

These restaurants have earned a *Wine Spectator* grand award (meaning it's the highest award given to restaurants that show a passion for the quality of their wine program) in 2008.

PATINA

www.patinagroup.com/patina
141 South Grand Avenue, Los Angeles, CA 90012
(213) 972-3331

Offers luxury dining in L.A.'s Walt Disney Hall. An award winning wine list plus seasonal menus make this restaurant one to try.

SONA

www.sonarestaurant.com
401 North La Cienega Boulevard, Los Angeles, CA 90048
(310) 659-7708

The restaurant's wine list has over 2,000 options. Nice wine and food pairings. They secure fresh ingredients for their food. Interior is sophisticated.

VALENTINO

www.valentinorestaurant.com
3115 Pico Boulevard, Santa Monica CA 90405
(310) 829-4313

Valentino's wine list contains over 2,500 wines and focuses on Italian cuisine.

Wine Spectator award of excellence restaurant

CUT
www.wolfgangpuck.com
9500 Wilshire Boulevard, Beverly Hills, CA 90212
(310) 276-8500

A Wolfgang Puck restaurant focusing on steak. Nice list of California wine options.

Unique Wine Restaurant

CRAFT
www.craftrestaurant.com/craft_losangeles_style.html
10100 Constellation Boulevard, Los Angeles, CA 90067
(310) 279-4180

Focusing on local, fresh produce with an a la carte menu. The wine list has over 400 offerings

Wine Shop

THE WINE HOUSE
www.winehouse.com
2311 Cotner Avenue, Los Angeles, CA 90064
(800) 626-9463

Offers a huge selection of domestic and international wines and has been in business for over 30 years. They offer wine education classes, have a food section and experienced professionals are available to help you.

Lodging-Pampering

MALIBU BEACH INN
www.malibubeachinn.com
22878 Pacific Coast Highway, Malibu, CA 90265
(310) 456-6444

Located on the exclusive Billionaire's Beach, there are rooms with views of the ocean.

Lodging-Moderate

THE STANDARD
www.standardhotels.com/los-angeles
550 South Flower at Sixth Street, Los Angeles, CA 90071
(213) 892-8080
Modern, sleek and fun with prices that seem reasonable considering the cool atmosphere.

DOUBLETREE GUEST SUITES SANTA MONICA HOTEL
www.santamonicasuites.doubletree.com
1707 Fourth Street, Santa Monica, CA 90401 (310) 395-3332

MARRIOTT RESIDENCE INN
www.marriott.com,
1177 South Beverly Drive, Los Angeles, CA 90035
(310) 228-4100

Malibu

Malibu can be reached from the 101 freeway, exiting at Kanan Road. Just past the freeway exit and on the right hand side of the street, as you head toward the beach, is a shopping center that houses TIFA Chocolate, wine and chocolate pairings, and Stone Ground Breads. You'll want to stop at both of these shops to purchase snacks for your tasting adventure.

Where To Buy Items For A Picnic Basket

TIFA CHOCOLATE & GELATO
www.tifachocolate.com
5013 Kanan Road, Agoura Hills, CA 91301
(818) 879-0685

Sells chocolates from small producers all over the world. Hosts private chocolate tasting parties for at least five people and sometimes offers open tastings of chocolate and the how-to's on tasting chocolate.

STONE GROUND BREADS
www.stonegroundbreads.com
5005 Kanan Road, Agoura Hills, CA 91301
(818) 597-8774

Offers homemade breads like jalapeno, sesame egg and fresh bakery items like croissants, cupcakes and soft biscotti.

Malibu
Wine Focused Restaurant

MOONSHADOWS

www.moonshadowsmalibu.com

20356 Pacific Coast Highway, Malibu, CA 90265

(310) 456-3010

Offering a hip atmosphere, Moonshadows overlooks the ocean. Seafood is an emphasis on the menu.

Los Angeles Wineries

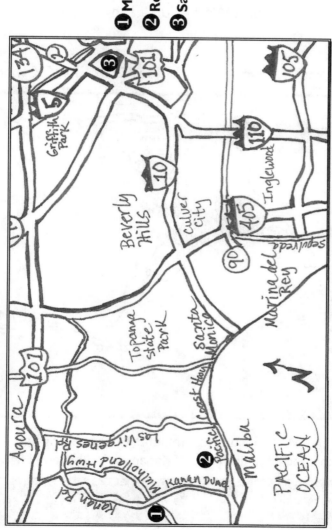

1 Malibu Family Wines
2 Rosenthal, Malibu Estate
3 San Antonio Winery

malibu wines

31800 Mulholland Highway
Malibu, California 90265

Open Wed - Sun 11am - 6pm

Proudly serving *Semler* & **SADDLEROCK** wines

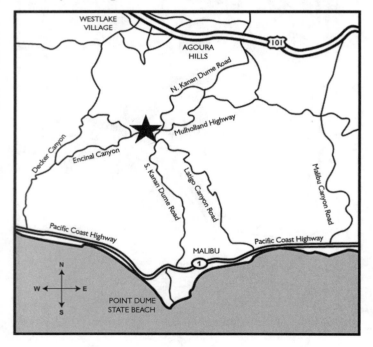

Wine Tasting just minutes from Los Angeles!
Located 1/2 Mile West of Kanan on Mulholland Highway

Malibu Family Wines

Most Southern California wineries boast that they are family owned but that usually means a husband and wife team. The Semler family, owners of Malibu Family Wines, incorporates the children too with eight of the nine siblings living on the property and most of them working there. The crew help manage the 1,000-acre Saddlerock Ranch estate located in the hills of Malibu's Santa Monica Mountains. The winery grows grapes on 65 acres of the property in their own Saddle Rock-Malibu AVA. Their Semler brand uses 100% estate grown grapes and between 5,000 and 8,000 cases of wine are produced a year. The '05 Semler Merlot received a Gold award from the San Francisco Chronicle Wine Competition. The tasting room is located a few miles from the estate at Malibu wines.

 TASTING ROOM LOCATION: 31800 Mulholland Highway, Malibu, CA 90265 (888) 433-9463 or (818) 865-0605

 WEBSITE: www.malibufamilywines.com

 HOURS: Wednesday through Sunday 11 a.m. to 6 p.m.

 TOURS: Yes, by appointment

 TASTING CHARGE: Yes

 WINE FOCUS: Cabernet Sauvignon, Merlot, Sauvignon Blanc and Syrah varietals

 DIRECTIONS: Take the 101 toward Malibu to Kanan Road. Head Southwest toward beach on Kanan. Kanan becomes CR-N9. Make slight right at Mulholland Highway. Tasting room is about a half mile from the turn.

Rosenthal
The Malibu Estate

The tasting room for Rosenthal is located on the beautiful Pacific Coast Highway overlooking Malibu beach and is owned by George Rosenthal, owner of Raleigh Enterprises. The Rosenthal Estate wines are from 100% Malibu Newton Canyon Appellation estate grapes, however, the wines are made in San Luis Obispo. The estate grows vines on 27 hilly acres. Their first commercial vintage was in 2001. The winery also produces a Surf Rider brand that contributes $1 a bottle toward the Surf Rider foundation. The winery makes about 5,000 cases a year of the estate wines. Their '99 Merlot won a double Gold medal at the Tasters Guild International Wine Judging, a Gold from the Los Angeles County Fair Wine Competition and a Silver from the San Francisco Chronicle Wine Competition to name a few.

 TASTING ROOM LOCATION: 26023 Pacific Coast Highway, Malibu CA 90265 (310) 456-1392

 WEBSITE: www.rosenthalestatewines.com

 HOURS: Wednesday through Sunday 11 a.m. to 6 p.m.

 TOURS: Yes, by appointment

 **TASTING CHARGE:** Yes

WINE FOCUS: Estate grown Bordeaux

 DIRECTIONS: Take the 101 toward Malibu and exit at either the Las Virgenes Road or Kanan Road exit and head toward Pacifc Coast Highway.

San Antonio Winery

Set amid buildings in downtown Los Angeles, San Antonio's ivy-covered walls only hint at what is revealed inside. Once indoors, the atmosphere turns sophisticated. You'll find a tasting bar and a large-stocked gift section with wine barrels surrounding the restaurant's dining area. They have everything from sandwiches to pastas.

The Los Angeles area had one of the first commercial growers, Joseph Chapman, in the 1820s. San Antonio Winery hints toward that history. You'll find a marker near the entrance citing the winery as a "City of Los Angeles Cultural Historical Landmark." Santo Cambianica began San Antonio Winery in 1917. His nephew, Stefano Riboli, continued the tradition and today it is still owned by the same family. Although there are no vineyards at the winery, the family owns vineyards in Napa Valley and elsewhere and makes their wine from grapes grown there. The Wine Enthusiast rated their '01 Riboli Cabernet Sauvignon 90 points.

 LOCATION: 737 Lamar Street, Los Angeles, California 90031 (323) 223-1401

 WEBSITE: www.sanantoniowinery.com

 HOURS: Open daily (except major holidays) 10 a.m. to 6 p.m.

 TOURS: Yes, on the hour from 12 noon to 4 p.m.

 TASTING CHARGE: No

 WINE FOCUS: Fine Wines

 DIRECTIONS: You'll see the signs for the winery off I-5. Head toward Los Angeles on I-5. At North Main Street, near the 110 freeway, head west, then make a left at Lamar.

Rancho Cucamonga Wineries

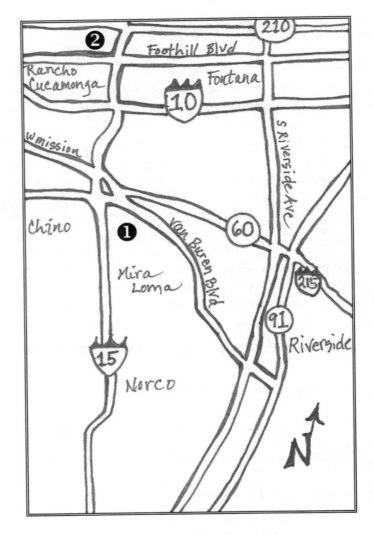

❶ Galleano Winery

❷ Joseph Filippi Winery

Galleano Winery

Galleano Winery sits in a place unlikely for one. Hidden among office warehouses and surrounded by dusty freeways, the winery is like a fort staking claim to its history. Its rustic buildings are a nod to early America; in fact, the 1890s two-story home on the property still houses the Galleano family. As you drive toward the winery you'll notice what look like neglected grape vines. However, the grapes from those vines are sought after by wineries all over California because they're considered "old vine" wine grapes. Their average age is 90. They look neglected because they "dry farm" the grapes (meaning that they don't add a single drop of water to them other than normal rainfall). The winery is named a historic winery by the National Register of Historic Places and California Register of Historical Resources. It has been making wine since 1933.

Their 2000 Zinfandel Port won a Gold in the Orange County Fair Wine Competition and Chairman's Award Long Beach Wine Competition. Their Syrah Port won a Gold at the Orange County, San Diego, Jerry Mead and Long Beach competitions.

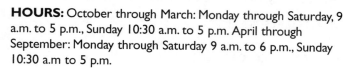

LOCATION: 4231 Wineville Road, Mira Loma, California 91752 (951) 685-5376

WEBSITE: www.galleanowinery.com

HOURS: October through March: Monday through Saturday, 9 a.m. to 5 p.m., Sunday 10:30 a.m. to 5 p.m. April through September: Monday through Saturday 9 a.m. to 6 p.m., Sunday 10:30 a.m to 5 p.m.

TOURS: Yes, weekends between 2 and 4 p.m.

TASTING CHARGE: No

WINE FOCUS: Zinfandel and Port

DIRECTIONS: Take I-15 toward Rancho Cucamonga to the Limonite exit. Head east. Make a left at Wineville Road.

Joseph Filippi Winery

Joseph Filippi Winery is set among a backdrop of hilly mountains and a few vineyards. Their upscale tasting room is very large and is well stocked with a wide range of gift items. You'll find the wine tasting bar near the back and an art gallery on the second floor.

The winery also has a tasting room in Ontario at Guasti near the Ontario airport. The area was founded in 1900 and used to be a working winery but now is more of a tourist location with a historic Mission Revival villa completed in 1923. The estate includes della robia reliefs, frescos, a marble statuary and European furniture. There's a bakery and café on the premises featuring pastries, sandwiches and a European-style menu.

The winery is family owned and has been in the hands of a long line of Filippis. They purchased the current Rancho Cucamonga site—a historical landmark claimed to be the oldest winery in California (formerly called Thomas Winery) – in 1965.

 LOCATION: Winery - 12467 Base Line Road, Rancho Cucamonga, California 91739 (909) 899-5755
Tasting Room - 2803 East Guasti Road, Ontario, California 91743 (909) 390-6998

 WEBSITE: www.josephfilippiwinery.com

 HOURS: Monday through Thursday, 10 a.m. to 5 p.m., Saturday, 10 a.m to 6 p.m. and Sunday 11 a.m. to 5 p.m.

 TOURS: Yes

 TASTING CHARGE: Yes

 WINE FOCUS: Premium wines

 DIRECTIONS: To the winery: Take I-15 toward Barstow/Las Vegas. At Base Line Road in Rancho Cucamonga, head west. The winery is on the left. To the Ontario tasting room: Take the I-10 freeway (east if you're coming from Los Angeles, west if you're coming from San Diego). Exit at Archibald Avenue and head south. Head east on Guasti Drive. The tasting room is on the left.

Antelope Valley

The Antelope Valley hosts over 40 vineyards although currently there are just five wine tasting venues. The area is seeking to get their own appellation and includes the Leona Valley which has secured their own appellation. In about an hour's drive from Los Angeles you can discover Agua Dulce Winery, Leona Valley Winery, Antelope Valley Winery and Cameo Winery. A little further drive north takes you to Souza Family Vineyards in Tehachapi.

A few miles from Agua Dulce Canyon Road is **Sweet Water Farms, 33301 Agua Dulce Canyon Road, Agua Dulce CA 91390 (661) 268-0700.** You'll find snacks like beef jerky, hazelnuts, sunflower seeds and deli sandwiches with fresh cookies.

Antelope Valley Wine Focused Restaurants

LE CHENE RESTAURANT

www.lechene.com
At 12625 Sierra Highway, Agua Dulce, California 91390
(661) 251-4315

Offers French Provencal cuisine, named "Best of Award of Excellence" from *Wine Spectator* and has four wine cellars. Occasionally the restaurant holds wine tastings. Open for dinner and Sunday brunch.

Unique Restaurant
BISTRO ARGENTINE

858 W. Lancaster Blvd. Lancaster, CA 93534
93534 (661) 948-2253

Offers Argentine style meals with aspects of Spain, Italy, Germany, France and the Middle East. Leona Valley Wine is available here.

OXFORD SUITES

www.oxfordsuiteslancaster.com
1651 West Avenue K, Lancaster, CA 93534
(661) 949-3423

Offers wine tour packages.
Reasonable rates in nice surroundings.

Limo Services

DESERT STARS LIMOUSINE

(661) 940-1914

Private (4- and 8-hour) tours to vineyards and wineries throughout the Antelope Valley.

Vineyards and Wine Tasting one hour from downtown Los Angeles.

Wine Tasting in Southern California.
North of Los Angeles is a vibrant winegrowing community. The Antelope Valley Winegrowers Association wants you to know about this great winemaking region.
Visit our website for Winery and Vineyard listings.

www.avwinegrowers.org

Antelope Valley Wineries

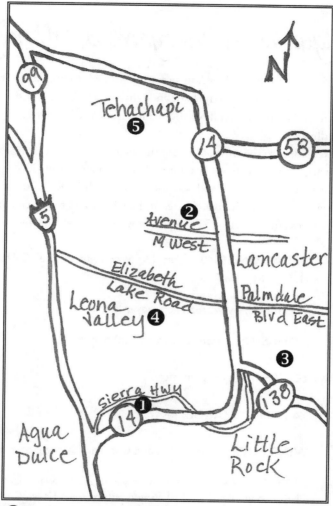

1 Agua Dulce Vineyards & Winery

2 Antelope Valley Winery

3 Cameo Ranch & Winery

4 Leona Valley Winery

5 Souza Family Vineyards

Agua Dulce Vineyards & Winery

The drive up Sierra Highway takes you through rolling hills. Grape vines sit prettily next to the barn and ranch-style building. Inside the tasting room the open ceilings reveal piping and a loft area to view the bottling.

According to the wine attendant the area has perfect conditions for growing grapes, with temperatures that fluctuate about 30 degrees from morning to night and soil that has a slightly acidic structure. They grow six varieties on 90 acres at the winery and make wine from the grapes grown there. 25,000 cases of wine are produced a year.

 LOCATION: 9640 Sierra Highway, Agua Dulce, California 91390 (661) 268-7402

 WEBSITE: www.aguadulcevineyards.com

 HOURS: Open from 10 a.m. to 5:30 p.m daily

 TOURS: Yes, by appointment

 TASTING CHARGE: Yes

 WINE FOCUS: Sangiovese and Cabernet Sauvignon

 DIRECTIONS: Take the I-5 freeway headed toward Santa Clarita, then take the 14 freeway north to Agua Dulce Canyon Road. Turn left. After about 3 miles, make a left at the continuation of Agua Dulce Canyon Road.

Antelope Valley Winery

This winery makes wine from grapes grown in the Antelope Valley and supports a number of growers that don't currently have a tasting room. Expect to see more tasting rooms in the future. For now, if you want a sampling of what this soon-to-be appellation produces, it's best to stop by here. Don't expect fancy surroundings. But, you'll find attendants that know their stuff when it comes to making wine. Stainless steel and barrel storage are in the back of the winery with a no-nonsense room that's available for events. Some of their recent awards include a Silver for the '05 Tempranillo, a Bronze for their '06 Chardonnay and a Bronze for their '04 Fusion, all from the '07 American Wine Society International Wine Competition. They produce from 5,000 to 6,000 cases a year.

 LOCATION: 42041 20th Street West, Lancaster, California 93534 (661) 722-0145

 WEBSITE: www.avwinery.com

HOURS: Open daily, 11 a.m. to 6 p.m.

 TOURS: Yes, by appointment

TASTING CHARGE: Yes

WINE FOCUS: Fruit forward reds

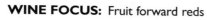
 DIRECTIONS: From the Los Angeles area head North on I-5 to the 14 North. Exit Avenue M. Turn left one block to 20th Street West. Turn right on 20th Street West. Winery is on the left side on the corner of 20th Street West and Avenue M.

Cameo Ranch & Winery

The Godde family were pioneers in the Antelope valley in the 1880s. They started out as farmers (there's even a Godde pass landmark in the area) and grew almonds, wheat and grapes back then. Generations later, Steve Godde, the current owner, came back from school at UC Davis and decided to bring back grapes to the Antelope Valley. This was in the 1980s and their first commercial harvest was in 1986. Steve had started a trend.

The winery showcases wines that are representative of the area. All the grapes used in the wine are from the Antelope Valley. Some of the wines they produce are Syrah, Sangiovese, Treviano and Symphony. Good bets here are the sweet Muscat and Symphony. The tasting room is located inside a building called Charley Brown Farms, a mercantile store that offers stuff like BBQ sandwiches and milkshakes.

 TASTING ROOM LOCATION: 8317 Pearblossom Highway, Littlerock, California 93589 (661) 944-3151

 WEBSITE: www.cameovineyards.com

 HOURS: Thursday through Monday 1 to 7 p.m.

 TOURS: No

 TASTING CHARGE: Yes

 WINE FOCUS: Reds

 DIRECTIONS: Take I-5 North to the 14 freeway toward Antelope Valley. Exit at Santiago Road and head South. Make a left at Sierra Highway and merge right at Pearblossom.

Leona Valley Winery

A new wine appellation sitting between Agua Dulce and Antelope Valley is Leona Valley. The Leona Valley Winery is the top producer in the area sitting on 50 acres—20 of them planted with grape vines. The green-tipped rolling hills lined with a valley of scattered buildings are reminiscent of a small European village. The rustic tasting room at the winery reminds me of an adult version of the tree house my carpenter brother put together for us as kids. It's fitting for the way the winery feels so close to the earth. Eventually, there will be a full winery with a bed and breakfast on the property but I hope they keep that close to the earth feeling. The goddess wine labels that were painted by a local artist have renditions of women that work there. They produce 100% estate grown grapes. And, the winery sits on a fault line which is the name for another line of their wines. 5,000 cases are produced per year.

LOCATION: 40352 90th Street West, Leona Valley, California 93551 (661) 270-9463

WEBSITE: www.leonavalleywinery.com

TASTING ROOM HOURS: Saturday through Sunday, 1 to 7 p.m. by appointment

TOURS: By appointment

TASTING CHARGE: Yes

WINE FOCUS: Bordeaux style (Cabernet Franc, Petit Verdot, Malbec and Cabernet Sauvignon)

DIRECTIONS: Take I-5 North to the 14 freeway toward Antelope Valley. At Elizabeth Lake Road turn left and then left at 90th Street. Look for gates with a wagon wheel and a big red barn.

Souza Family Vineyards

On the border of Southern and Central California is the Souza Family Vineyards in Tehachapi about 45 minutes North of the Antelope Valley. Bob and Patty Souza moved to the area in 1990 from the San Fernando Valley and found that it was a good climate for the Primitivo Zinfandel grape and thus planted a vineyard. They're working on getting appellation status for the Tehachapi Valley. They grow the grapes on site but the wine is processed in Paso Robles and then sent back down to them so the wine is 100% estate grown. The first vines were planted in 2003 and already their '05 Primitivo Zinfandel won a Silver medal and their '06 Primitivo Zinfandel won a Bronze at the '08 San Francisco Chronicle Wine Competition.

 LOCATION: 26877 Cummings Valley Road, Tehachapi, California 93561 (661) 822-9233

 WEBSITE: www.souzafamilyvineyard.com

 TASTING ROOM HOURS: Friday through Sunday 11 a.m. to 6 p.m.

 TOURS: Yes, of grounds and vineyard

 TASTING CHARGE: Yes

 WINE FOCUS: Zinfandel

 DIRECTIONS: Take I-5 to 14 North, left at CA-58 toward Bakersfiield, last turnoff to Tehachapi Tucker Road.

Oxnard/Ventura

The Oxnard/Ventura winery region sits on the northern tip of the Southern California area. Some of the wineries source their grapes from the central coast growing areas.

Wine Focused Restaurants (Wine Spectator Awarded)

BROOKS

www.restaurantbrooks.com
545 East Thompson Boulevard, Ventura, CA 93001
(805) 652-7070

Creates Contemporary American cuisine using local seasonal ingredients. In the historic downtown district of Ventura near the ocean, in a rustic but modern setting.

CAFE FIORE

www.fiorerestaurant.net
66 California Street, Ventura, CA 93001
(805) 653-1266

In the downtown area, Fiore offers rustic Italian food in a comfortable and warm setting.

CAFE NOUVEAU

1497 East Thompson Boulevard, Ventura, CA 93001
(805) 648-1422

Known for their breakfast, they also offer lunch and dinner on some nights. Atmosphere is Art Deco style.

Unique Restaurants

ENOTECA TOSCANA WINE BISTRO
www.enotecatoscanawinebistro.com
2088 E. Ventura Blvd., Camarillo, CA 93010
(805) 445-1433

Focuses on Tuscan and Spanish dishes using fresh ingredients. Features large wine list by the glass and bottle. Open for lunch and dinner. Closed on Monday.

LA DOLCE VITA
www.theldv.com
740 South B. Street, Oxnard, CA 93030
(805) 486-6878

Creates Italian and Mediterranean fusion cuisine in an elegantly casual environment. Offers cooking classes. Open for lunch and dinner. Closed on Monday.

THE SIDECAR
www.thesidecarrestaurant.com
3029 E. Main Street, Ventura, CA 93003
(805) 653-7433

Using ingredients from local Ventura County Farms, the Sidecar makes seasonal, sophisticated cuisine in a relaxed atmosphere. Has brunch on Sunday and open for dinner. Closed Mondays.

Lodging

EMBASSY SUITES
www.mandalaybeach.embassysuites.com
2101 Mandalay Beach Road, Oxnard, CA 93035
(805) 984-2500

Situated on the ocean, it offers the standard suite rooms all Embassy Suites offer.

Pampering

OJAI VALLEY INN & SPA
www.ojairesort.com
905 Country Club Road, Ojai, CA 93023
(800) 422-6524

An 80 year-old resort and spa only a few minutes from the Casa Barranca winery.

Oxnard/Ventura Wineries

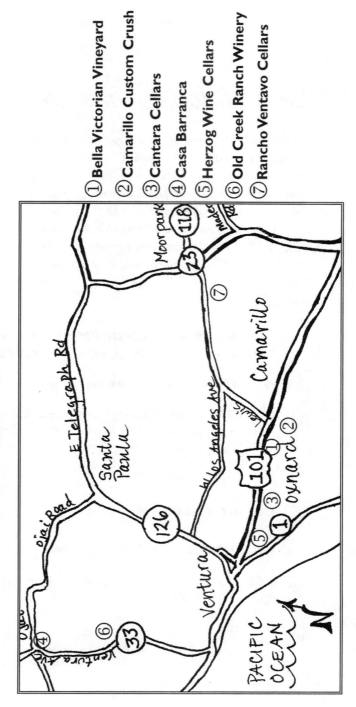

① Bella Victorian Vineyard
② Camarillo Custom Crush
③ Cantara Cellars
④ Casa Barranca
⑤ Herzog Wine Cellars
⑥ Old Creek Ranch Winery
⑦ Rancho Ventavo Cellars

Bella Victorian Vineyard

Bella Victorian Vineyard is a boutique winery with a theme of romance. Owned by Jerry and Kimberly Monahan, you'll find weddings a main focus at the private Victorian Vineyard.

At the boutique, lingerie, books, handbags and accessories are sold. The tasting room, located in the old town of Camarillo, offers wine flights paired with fusion bistro small plate foods made by their French chef. The theme is Victorian homey and old world.

Vineyards are by appointment only at the private estate in Camarillo. The *Wine Spectator* rated the 2004 Cuvee (Cab and Merlot blend) 91 points.

 TASTING ROOM LOCATION: 2135 East Ventura Boulevard, Camarillo, California 93010 (805) 383-8800

 WEBSITE: www.bellavictorianvineyard.com

 TASTING ROOM HOURS: Monday through Wednesday, Thursday through Saturday, 11 a.m. to 8 p.m., Sunday 11 a.m. to 6 p.m.

 TOURS: Yes, by appointment

 TASTING CHARGE: Yes

 WINE FOCUS: Cuvee 91, Syrah and Pinot

 DIRECTIONS: Take 101, exit Lewis Road, turn right, turn right on Ventura Blvd.

Camarillo Custom Crush Winery

Camarillo Custom Crush Winery was started in 1972 as a private producer. Today, they primarily make wines for local growers and offer winemaking services to vineyard owners, restaurants and people interested in their own private boutique wine label winemaking services.

The tasting room and winery is in a large commercial building. They don't grow grapes here but they purchase grapes mostly from Southern California. Some of the wines they produce are Cabernet Sauvignon, Merlot, Syrah, Tempranillo, Petite Sirah and Zinfandel. The '06 Cielo Syrah won a Double Gold at San Francisco International.

 LOCATION: 300 South Lewis Road Suite C, Camarillo, California 93012 (805) 484-0597

 WEBSITE: www.camarillocustomcrush.com

 TASTING ROOM HOURS: Saturday to Sunday 11 a.m. to 5 p.m. Private tasting by appointment

 TOURS: Yes, by appointment

 TASTING CHARGE: Yes

 WINE FOCUS: Handcrafted Red Wine

 DIRECTIONS: Take 101 toward Camarillo and exit at the Lewis Road offramp.

Cantara Cellars

Cantara Cellars winery sits in a 5,000 square foot tasting room in an industrial park. The husband and wife team, Mike and Chris Brown, have been making wine since 2003. It started when Mike's parents bought 28 acres of Chardonnay vineyards in Lodi California and gave them some grapes. Later they purchased more grape varieties and increased their knowledge so today you can find varieties like Chardonnay, Zinfandel, Syrah, Tempranillo, Barbera and Petite Sirah.

 LOCATION: 126 Wood Road Suite 104, Camarillo, California 93010 (805) 484-9600

 WEBSITE: www.cantaracellars.com

 TASTING ROOM HOURS: Saturday to Sunday 11 a.m. to 5 p.m., Monday through Friday by appointment

 TOURS: Yes

 TASTING CHARGE: Yes

 WINE FOCUS: Lodi Appellation wines

 DIRECTIONS: Take the 101 toward Camarillo and exit at Central Avenue. Head South on Central to West Ventura Boulevard. Make a left. Take a right at Wood Road.

Casa Barranca

Casa Barranca is a certified organic winery and is located in a National Historic Landmark Estate that was originally designed in 1909. The wine facility is located in a "century-old subterranean stone water cistern". Old World skills were used to create the shelving in the cistern. They even get their water from an artesian spring and the building is powered with solar energy. They produce boutique, hand crafted wines made from grapes grown without pesticides or herbicides on their farm as well grapes they purchase elsewhere. Some of the varieties you'll find here are Pinot Noir, Grenache, Cabernet Sauvignon, Syrah, Viognier and Chardonnay.

 LOCATION: 208 East Ojai Avenue, Ojai, California 93023
(805) 640-1255

 WEBSITE: www.casabarranca.com

 TASTING ROOM HOURS: Thursday through Sunday,
12 p.m. to 6 p.m.

 TOURS: No

 TASTING CHARGE: Yes

 WINE FOCUS: Handcrafted Red Wines

 DIRECTIONS: Take the 101 toward Ojai, then 33 which
turns into North Ventura Avenue. Then, merge right on East
Ojai Avenue.

Herzog Wine Cellars

Housed in an industrial building next to other office suites is Herzog Wine Cellars in Oxnard. The tasting room, restaurant and self-guided tour of the winemaking process offers a marked contrast to the outside surroundings. Warm yellows and ochres on the walls and fine details inside the building draw you in. The Tierra Sur restaurant is housed next to the tasting bar and features Mediterranean influenced seasonal cuisine. Check the website for ongoing wine classes and events. The winery produces their wine from purchased grapes in central California. Their '05 Herzog Special Reserve Alexander Valley Cabernet Sauvignon received 90 points from Wine Enthusiast. Other awards include a best of class/Gold Medal from the Los Angeles International wine competition for their '05 Herzog Special Reserve Late Harvest White Riesling, 87 points from *Wine Spectator* for the '05 Baron Herzog Chardonnay and the list goes on.

 LOCATION: 3201 Camino Del Sol, Oxnard, California 92030 (805) 983-1560

 WEBSITE: www.herzogwinecellars.com

 TASTING ROOM HOURS: Sunday through Friday, 11 a.m. until restaurant closing.

 TOURS: Yes, self guided

 TASTING CHARGE: Yes

 WINE FOCUS: Kosher wines

 DIRECTIONS: From Highway 101, exit Del Norte and head South on Del Norte (toward the ocean). Turn right at the first street, Camino Del Sol. The winery is on the right hand side, just past the train tracks.

Old Creek Ranch Winery

Situated where southern California meets central California is Old Creek Ranch Winery. Owned by John and Carmel Whitman, it's been family owned and operated since 1981. With 850 acres of cattle ranch and numerous dogs, horses and sheep roaming the ranch, the owners encourage visitors to bring picnic baskets and spend the afternoon. Currently, the winery purchases grapes from central and northern California due to Pierce's Disease having destroyed their previous 20 acres of vines. They were recently awarded "Best of Ventura Wineries 2008" by the US Local Business Association and their 2003 Sangiovese won a double Gold from the San Francisco International wine festival. The winery produces 2,000 cases a year.

 LOCATION: 10024 Old Creek Road, Ventura, California 93001 (805) 649-4132

 WEBSITE: www.oldcreekranch.com

 HOURS: Open daily 11 a.m. to 5 p.m.

 TOURS: Yes

 TASTING CHARGE: Yes

 WINE FOCUS: Hand crafted, handmade wines that are true to their varietal.

 DIRECTIONS: Take 101 to the 33 North. The 33 turns into a two-lane highway. Pass through a small town called Casitas Springs. Turn right at Old Creek Road where there's a big red barn.

Rancho Ventavo Cellars

Owners George Gilpatrick and Faye Hawes started out as home winemakers in 1995. Their "out-of-control hobby" turned into a business in 2005 when George agreed to make the wine and Faye would sell it. Faye took years to find the perfect tasting room setting–a historic downtown Oxnard 1902 house. The comfy environment includes hardwood oak floors, glass doors and windows, and oak paneling. You'll find Cabernet Franc, Cabernet Sauvignon, Merlot, Pinot Noir, Petit Sirah, Tempranillo (popular according to Faye) Syrah plus Majecc (a blend of 10 varietals and named after their grandchildren) and Mouvedre wines. They source the grapes and produce 2,400 cases a year.

 TASTING ROOM LOCATION 741 South A Street, Oxnard, California 93030 (805) 483-8084

 WEBSITE: www.ranchoventavo.com

 HOURS: Thursday through Monday 10 a.m. to 6 p.m.

 TOURS: No

 TASTING CHARGE: Yes

 WINE FOCUS: Hardy Red Wines

 DIRECTIONS: Take Highway 1 toward Oxnard which turns into South Oxnard Boulevard. Make a left at West 8th Street and a right at South A Street.

Wine Clubs

Note: Most of the wineries listed in this book have wine clubs that will (for a fee) send you wine once a month. Check with the individual winery you are interested in.

AMERICAN INSTITUTE OF WINE AND FOOD (AIWF)
www.aiwf.org
This organization was founded by Julia Child and Robert Mondavi. Membership includes educational programs and events as well as newsletters and announcements of events. It's a national organization. Check website for a local chapter near you.

WINE OF THE MONTH CLUB
www.WineoftheMonthClub.com
Membership is free and open to everyone. For information, write to the club.
Wine of the Month Club
907 South Magnolia Avenue, Monrovia, California 91016
(800) 949-WINE

ORANGE COUNTY WINE SOCIETY
www.ocws.org
(714) 708-1636
A non-profit educational club to help members understand wine and winemaking, viticulture and appreciation. Has a home winemaker group.

INTERNATIONAL WINE & FOOD SOCIETY
www.iwfs.org
The worlds oldest epicurean society. Its mission is to promote knowledge and understanding of wine and food. It was started in 1933. There are branches throughout the United States. Check the website for a location near you.

Websites

Wine.com
www.wine.com
Provides information about wine pertaining to tasting wine, pairing food with wine, types of wine, a glossary, guides and resources. The site also sells wine by winery or growing region and by varietal.

The Wine Lovers Website
www.drinkwine.com
Includes information about wine and wineries, food, dining, references and a "how to" section.

Wine Online
www.wine.net
Features a wide selection of premium wine brands with a search engine by name, varietal, price or region.

Wine Spectator Magazine
www.winespectator.com
Includes daily wine news, features, library, dining, travel and more.

Wine Country Minute
www.winecountryminute.com
This website is for wine enthusiasts who want to stay updated and connected with the lifestyle of the wine country. They have a one-minute a day, three days a week free email. Most of their content focuses on the California wine country.

Sustainable Table
www.sustainabletable.org
Covers what you need to know to introduce healthy food choices into your life. Lists farmers' markets, restaurants, CSAs and other sustainable friendly businesses in your area.

Eco Wine

www.ecowine.com

An online wine shop offering "earth-friendly" wines from certified organically grown grapes.

Free the Grapes

www.freethegrapes.org

A grassroots organization for consumers, wineries and retailers to allow wine direct shipping. You can help change the laws so that it's easier to order wine from states that are still restricted, or send wine to those restricted states.

Local Wine Events

www.localwineevents.com

Features local wine events, dinners, cooking classes and related wine focused happenings in your area. An extensive and helpful listing of wine events in your area. You can sign up for their weekly newsletter featuring your area's food and drink events.

Vin Village

www.Vinvillage.com

A social organization established for networking with wine and food lovers in your hometown or anywhere in the U.S.

Taste of Wine TV

www.tasteofwinetv.com

Contains articles about local Southern California wineries, events and happenings as well as videos covering the events.

Glossary

Acidity
Term used to describe the sharpness or tartness of a wine. Acids are found in all grapes and occur in wine naturally. You will sense this taste after you've swallowed the wine. Your mouth will be dry and you will salivate.

Aeration
The act of exposing wine to oxygen. This process can soften a wine. Some people put wine in carafes to aerate it.

Aging
Term that describes the process of storing wine over time to allow it to adopt a softer, more complex taste. Wines are usually aged in a barrel or bottle and sometimes in both.

Appellation
Can be the name of a vineyard, county, or district. It defines where the grapes are grown. If a California wine label states an appellation, it must consist of at least 85 percent of wine from that area.

Aroma
Term used to describe the overall smell of wine.

Astringency
Caused by tannin in wine from seeds and skins of grapes. Creates a puckery feel in the mouth.

Balance
This term includes the flavor and texture of wine, including the sweetness, acidity, tannin, and alcohol that come together to create a wholeness.

Botrytis Cinerea
A type of mold that shrivels grapes, leaving their flavor stronger and their sugar content higher.

Body
Term used to describe how heavy the wine feels in the mouth. The more alcohol a wine has, the more body it seems to have.

Bouquet
The wine's smell, which becomes stronger as the wine ages.

Brut
Describes an especially dry sparkling wine.

Carbonic Maceration
A process where whole grapes and their stems are fermented together in a closed container. The grapes are then pressed to extract the wine. The wine produced tends to be light and fruity.

Claret
A British term describing a red wine from Bordeaux that is aged for years in barrels.

Clarification
Process of removing sediment from fermented wine.

Clarity
How clear the wine looks in the glass.

Cortese
A white wine that can be described as rich and dry. It consists of different types of grapes.

Decant
To get clear wine, wine is poured from the bottle into a container called a decanter so that the sediment stays in the bottle.

Earthy
When a wine is described as "earthy," its scent or taste is of things that are found in the earth (this term describes both good and bad qualities).

Fermentation
A step in the winemaking process. There are two types of fermentation processes. One is alcoholic fermentation (sugars turn into alcohol) and the other is malolactic fermentation (malic acid turns into lactic acid).

Finish
The final feeling or taste after wine is swallowed. It is the lasting impression after wine has been in the mouth. When the finish is agreeable, it leaves the mouth wanting more.

Generic
These wines tend to be less expensive than varietal wines and are a combination of grape varieties.

Grassy
A word used to describe a wine that has tastes or aromas of grass, hay, or a hint of vegetable. The term has both good and bad connotations, depending on the opinion of the taster.

Heat Summation
Term used in California to describe the best place to grow wine grapes determined by an area's average daily temperature from April to October. Once the average temperature is determined, the areas are designated from Region I for the coolest areas through Region V for the warmest ones.

Jammy
A term used to describe the taste of wine when it has a heavy, jam-like flavor.

Late Harvest
Wines produced from grapes that have been picked after the regular harvest season. This process makes the wines sweeter. Dessert wines are usually made from late harvest grapes.

Lees
Residue of different ingredients, like yeast and grape parts, remaining in barrels after the fermentation process.

Legs
A pattern obtained by swirling a glass of wine. The wine lingers on the glass, creating a leg-like pattern on the sides. People sometimes mistake this process as an indication of a wine's quality, but actually it's a measure of the alcohol content.

Length
A portion of the number of taste buds along the tongue that the wine reaches and the total time the aroma and taste last after drinking the wine.

Must
The combination of grape juice, pulp, and skin obtained through crushing.

Non-vintage
Wines that do not have a vintage year on the label and are often blends of grapes from various years.

Nose
The combination of grape aroma and bouquet of wine.

Reserve
This name is sometimes given to a bottle of varietal wine that is more expensive than the regular bottles with the same varietal name. There is no legal standard for this name, so the meaning can vary from one winery to the next. Usually these wines have more flavor and have been aged longer than regular wines.

Residual Sugar
The type of sugar that stays after the wine ferments.

Sommelier
A person who is in charge of wines.

Sur Lie

A French saying that translates as "on the lees." This is an aging procedure where wines stay in contact with the dead yeast cells after fermentation.

Sweetness

This term is used to describe what the tongue experiences when tasting wine. Wines that have a sugary taste are given this term.

Tannin

In the skins, seeds, and stem of grapes, an antioxidant that slows the aging process of wine. Red wines have more tannin than white wines because they are fermented with their skins. Tannins act like a preservative and are the reason why red wines last (they are a crucial ingredient in aging wine). Tannin creates a "mouth puckery" reaction when tasted and leaves the mouth feeling dry.

Varietal

Wines made from one grape. For example, when a wine is labeled "Chardonnay," it must consist of 75 percent of that grape variety.

Vintage

Term to describe the harvesting year of the grape. When there is a vintage date on a bottle of wine, at least 95 percent of the grapes must be from that year.

Viscosity

Term used to describe wine's weight. Sometimes wine is described as watery, medium weight, heavy, or oily. This is the viscosity.

Viticultural Area/American Viticultural Area (AVA)

A type of appellation where winegrowers in certain areas will ask the government to grant them the right to put that area's name on their wine labels. If the right is granted, 85 percent of the wine in those bottles must be from that area.

Yeasty

Term used to describe the smell of yeast that may be likened to the smell of baking bread.

For Further
Reading/Sources

Adams, Leon D. *The Commonsense Book of Wine*,
New York: McGraw-Hill, 1986.

Austerman, John. *Baja California*, Los Angeles:
Automobile Club of Southern California, 1991.

Barrow, Clare. *Julian,* San Diego's North County Magazine,
Fall 1997.

Bernstein, Cal. *Wine! The Complete CD-ROM Guide*,
March 1997.

Bespaloffs, Alexis. *Complete Guide to Wine*, New York:
Penguin Books, 1994.

Boone, Jessica. *Our Favorite Wine Bars Near You*, Sunset
Magazine, June 2004

De Lude, Michelle. *California Winery Tours*, Los Angeles:
Travel Publications Department, Automobile Club of
Southern California, 1993.

Elwood, Ann. *Wineries, San Diego County and Temecula
Valley*, Los Angeles: Chalk Press, 1999.

Ewing-Mulligan, Mary. *Entertaining—Wine Tasting 101*. Martha
Stewart Living, May 1996.

Gaiter, Dorothy J. and John Brecher. "Giving American Rosés a Second Chance," *Wall Street Journal*, July 21, 1999.

Gaiter, Dorothy J. and John Brecher. *The Wall Street Journal Guide to Wine*, New York: Random House, 1999

Gaona, Elena. "Quiet Comeback," *San Diego Union Tribune*, June 25, 2006.

Geiser, Angela. "Gioveto, Cortese & Viognier—Temecula Wineries Shift Focus to Mediterranean Wines," *The Daily Californian*, April 28, 1996.

Gleeson, Bill. *Backroad Wineries of Southern California, a Scenic Tour of California Country Wineries*, San Francisco: Chronicle Books, 1994.

Goldberg, Howard. "The Best White Wine of All?" *Saveur Magazine*, May/June 1996.

Green, Richard. "Wine Drinkers Who Bother to Look at the Cork May Find Plastic," *San Diego Union-Tribune*, October 5, 1997.

San Diego Union-Tribune, "L.A. Count set to lift Prohibition-era ban on winemaking, July 31, 2000

Johnson, Hugh. *The World Atlas of Wine—The Wine Book of The Century*, New York: Simon and Schuster, 1985.

Kornblum, Annette. "Should You Drink to Your Health?" *Better Homes and Gardens*, October 1997.

MacNeil, Karen. "The Wine Guide." *Sunset Magazine* (every issue).

MacNeil, Karen. "Wine Tasting Porch Pics." *Cooking Light*, April 1999.

McCarthy, Ed. *Wine For Dummies*, Foster City, California: IDG Books Worldwide, 1995.

Marsano, Bill. "The Grace of a Civilized Table." *Weight*

Martin, Leslie. "The Puzzling Petite Sirah." *Country Living*, October 1997.

Parker, Robert. "California Bargains—Bottles from Top Wineries for $10 and Under." *Food & Wine Magazine*, May 1996.

Rhodes, Bob and Cindy, *The Grape Escapes 2*, Indianapolis, Dog Ear Publishing, 2008

Seff, Marsha Kay. "Julian, San Diego's Big Apple," *San Diego Union-Tribune*, October 20, 1996.

South Coast Wine Magazine

Staggs, Bill. "Why Wine is Really Better: New Research Shows the Fruit of the Vine is Rich in Compounds that Boost Alcohol's Benefits and May Dampen its Risks," *Health Magazine*, January–February 1996.

Steiman, Harvey. *Setting Its Own Pace—My 12 favorite Los Angeles restaurants celebrate the city's culinary diversity*, Wine Spectator, March 31, 2009.

Sunset Guide to California's Wine Country, Menlo Park, California: Lane Books, 1982.

Tarbell, Nick. "Grape Expectations—Recipe For a Wine Tasting," *Arizona Foothills*, April 1999.

Thompson, Bob and Hugh Johnson. *The California Wine Book*, 1976.

Wheelock, Walt and Gulick, Howard. *Baja California Guidebook—a Descriptive Traveler's Guide,* Glendale, California: Arthur H. Clark Co. 1980.

Whitley, Robert. "Crystal Persuasion Not Just Any Glass," *San Diego Union-Tribune*, May 29, 1997.

A

A.O.C, 133
Accidental Winery, 45
Acidity, 170
Aeration, 170
Adams, John Quincy, 16
Addison, 39, 55
Adobe Vineyards, 45
Aging, 170
Aglianico, 78
Agua Dulce Winery, 152
Aleatico, 21
Alex's Red Barn Winery, 92, 93
Almond Champagne, 122
Amante, 101
Amarillo Road Vineyard, 45
American Institute of Wine and
    Food, 167
American Viticultural Areas,
20, 45, 75, 174
Antelope Valley, 149
Antelope Valley Wineries, 151
Antelope Valley Winery, 151, 153
Antioxidants, 12
Appellation, 1, 20, 149, 155
Arneis, 79
Aroma, 170
Arroyo Dulce Cellars, 45
Art & Wine Festival, 71
Astringency, 170
Atwood Estate Vineyard, 82

B

Baby Lamb Chops, 42
Bacaro L.A., 133
Bailey, Drue, 50

Bailey, Frank, 50
Baily Vineyard & Winery, 92, 94
Baked Brie, 29
Balance, 171
Barbera, 21, 121, 162
Barbeque Pork Ribs, 32
Balboa Food and Wine School, 9
Baron's The Marketplace, 90
Barret Bird's Santa Margarita
Winery, 82
Bella Vista, 92, 95
Bella Victorian Vineyard, 159, 160
Bellefleur Restaurant, 56
Belle Marie Winery, 61, 62
Benefits of Wine, 12
Bernardo Winery, 61, 63
Best Western, 83
Bistro Argentine, 149
Blind Wine Tasting, 2
Block Five Restaurant at
Leonesse Winery, 88
Bodega Wine Bar, 134
Body, 171
Boorman Vineyards, 91
Bordeaux, 25, 94, 115, 144
Bouquet, 171
Botrytis Cinerea, 171
Brady, Thomas, 50
Bread & Cie, 59
Briar Rose, 92, 96
Brooks, 157
Broquer Vineyards, 45
Burgundy, 63
Butter Baked King Crab, 39

C

Cabernet Franc, 64, 66, 79, 91, 96, 104, 113, 118, 155, 166
Cabernet Sauvignon, 21, 62, 64, 66, 70, 71, 74, 77, 79, 80, 91, 93, 96, 100, 104, 121, 129, 143, 145, 152, 155, 161, 163, 164, 166
Cabernet-Mouverdre, 98
Cactus Star Vineyard, 45
Café Champagne at Thornton Winery, 88, 120
Café Fiore, 157
Café Nouveau, 157
California Taste Fine Wine, 126
Callaway Vineyard and Winery, 92, 97
Camarillo Custom Crush, 159
Cameo Ranch & Winery, 151, 154
Cantara Cellars, 159, 162
Carignane, 21, 63, 67
Carol's Restaurant, 88
Carlsbad, 47
Carlsbad Coastal Winery, 45
Carlsbad Company Stores, 47
Carlsbad Inn, 47
Carson Vineyard, 45
Casa Barranca, 159, 163
Century Tubes, 45
Chablis, 63
Champagnes, 120
Chapin Family Vineyards, 91
Chapman, Joseph, 145
Chardonnay, 21, 74, 81, 107, 118, 121, 153, 162, 163, 164
Chateau Viognier, 45

Chenin Blanc, 22
Chinnok Cellars Vineyards, 45
Chuao Chocolatier, 60
Chuparosa Vineyards, 45
Churon Winery, The Inn at Churon, 92, 98
Cinsault, 22
Citronier, 96
Claret, 171
Clarification, 171
Clarity, 171
Color, 8
Comfort Inn, 83
Community Building, 3
Community Supported Agriculture, 5
Concord, 63
Cordiano Winery, 61, 64
Cork Bar, 134
Cortese, 112
Cougar Vineyard, 92, 99
Counoise, 113
Cowper Family Vineyards, 82
Cuyamaca Mountains, 50
Craft, 137
Creekside Grille at Wilson Creek Winery, 88, 122
Cut, 137

D

Decant, 171
Decanter Wine Lounge and Restaurant, 52
Deer Park Winery, 61, 65
De Luz Farms, 5
Desert Stars Limousine, 150

The Five "S's" of Wine Tasting
Courtesy of Frank Mangio, *Taste of Wine TV*   *TasteOfWineTV.com*

Sight. Pour a small amount of wine in your stemmed glass and hold it by the stem. Focus on the color, intensity and clarity, while tilting the glass.

Swirl. Rest the glass on a table and rotate the wrist. Notice the wine on the side of the glass and the film it leaves. It's called the wine's "legs." A thicker "leg" means higher alcohol. You are also aerating the wine with oxygen, enhancing the taste to come.

Smell. Get your nose inside the glass, close to the wine and strongly inhale. The sensations rush through your sinuses and set up the palate with the penetrating aromas.

Sip. Slowly drink in the wine, making sure your entire mouth is flooded so that all your taste buds are getting saturated. Let the fruit, tannins and alcohol work their magic by "chewing" and sloshing it around the palate before the final "S" comes into play...

Swallow. The finish of a wine can last up to a minute or more depending on its body and vintage. It's a moment of meditation and satisfaction that only wine can create.

Order Form

Mail to:

Popcorn Press & Media, Janene Roberts, P.O. Box 3375
San Diego, CA 92067

Please send _____ copies of *Wine Tasting in Southern California &
Beyond* to:

Name:_____

Address:_____

City:_____ State:_____ ZIP:_____-_____

Telephone: (____) _____

Cost: # of books____@$15.95 $_____
$15.95 each

Sales Tax: Sales tax $_____
A 8.25% sales tax applies only if book is being sent to a California
address.

Shipping ($2.25 per book):   Shipping & Handling $_____
(Please allow three to four weeks for delivery)
Air mail rate is $4 to arrive within one week.

Please enclose payment. **TOTAL ENCLOSED** $_____

Order Today!

Tasting Notes

Name of Wine	Winery

Vintage	Date of Tasting	Price

Color

This is where you record the **Clarity** (How defined is the wine?), **Depth** (How mild or deep is it?), **Color** (If the wine is white, does it look yellow or brown? If the wine is red, does it have hints of purple or brown?), and **Viscosity** (Is the wine mild, average weight, weighty, or slick?)

Smell

Here's where you record the **Appearance** (Is the wine indefinite, distinct, noteworthy?), **Aroma** (Positive or negative?), and **Bouquet** (Is there one? Is it agreeable, involved, or strong?)

Taste

List here the **Sweetness** (Sweet or dry?), **Tannin** (Does it have it?), **Acidity**, **Body**, **Length**, and **Balance**.

Tasting Notes

Name of Wine

Winery

Vintage

Date of Tasting

Price

Color

This is where you record the **Clarity** (How defined is the wine?), **Depth** (How mild or deep is it?), **Color** (If the wine is white, does it look yellow or brown? If the wine is red, does it have hints of purple or brown?), and **Viscosity** (Is the wine mild, average weight, weighty, or slick?)

Smell

Here's where you record the **Appearance** (Is the wine indefinite, distinct, noteworthy?), **Aroma** (Positive or negative?), and **Bouquet** (Is there one? Is it agreeable, involved, or strong?)

Taste

List here the **Sweetness** (Sweet or dry?), **Tannin** (Does it have it?), **Acidity**, **Body**, **Length**, and **Balance**.